Leadership **Blurbs**

Bite Sized Strategies for a Growing Church

by Bob Franquiz

Leadership Blurbs: Bite Sized Strategies for a Growing Church

© Copyright 2014 by Fuel Media Group, Inc.

ISBN Number: 978-0-9772047-6-2

Library of Congress Control Number: 2014942153

Fuel Media Group, Inc.

14601 SW 29th St. #108

Miramar, FL 33027

All rights reserved. No part of this publication may be reproduced, stored in a retrieval system, or transmitted in any form or by any means – electronic, mechanical, photocopy, recording, or any other – except for brief quotations in written reviews, without the prior written permission of the publisher.

Scripture quotations marked (NKJV™) are taken from the New King James Version®. Copyright © 1982 by Thomas Nelson, Inc. Used by permission. All rights reserved.

Scripture quotations marked (NLT) are taken from the Holy Bible, New Living Translation, copyright © 1996. Used by permission of Tyndale House Publishers, Inc., Wheaton, Illinois 60189. All rights reserved.

Scripture quotations marked (NIV) are taken from the HOLY BIBLE, NEW INTERNATIONAL VERSION®. NIV®. Copyright©1973, 1978, 1984 by International Bible Society. Used by permission of Zondervan. All rights reserved.

Edited by Susan Andres

Cover Design by Mark Rodriguez

Interior Design by PlainJoe Studios

Back Cover Photo by Brian Rodriguez

Printed in the United States of America

10 9 8 7 6 5 4

"Bob Franquiz writes with raw honesty and creativity. His insight will make you dream. His humor will make you laugh. This book will help you become a better leader."

- Mark Batterson
Lead Pastor, National Community Church
Author, The Circle Maker

"Warning--you might not like this book; in fact, if you are searching for the latest and greatest formula as to how to grow your ministry you will probably throw it across the room. This is not a book written on "how" to do ministry--but rather "what" questions that ministry leaders should be asking. The things written about are easy to underline and highlight... but will be challenging to apply. Thanks Bob for writing a book that both encouraged me in some things and kicked me in the teeth in others...I loved it!"

- Perry Noble, Senior Pastor, NewSpring Church

"Bob has been in church leadership long enough to know the good, the bad and the ugly that accompanies it. "Leadership Blurbs" is great because it offers wisdom and inspiration to church pastors and leaders in 65 palpable, bite-size chunks."

- Troy Gramling, Lead Pastor at Potential Church

"I don't have much room for theory, and you won't find much in this book. It is down-to-earth and practical-you might even say it is simply strategic. It would be impossible for any pastor or church leader to not find a few transformational nuggets within these pages-I sure did."

-Tim Stevens, Leading Smart.com, Executive Pastor, Granger Community Church

"Leadership Blurbs is a fantastic book filled with practical wisdom and insights that apply to both church planters and ministry veterans alike! Bob goes beyond just simply giving 'principles' and poses impacting questions that will help Pastors look within and evaluate their own personal leadership. This book is a must read for anyone who is passionate about growing a healthy, high impact church!"

-Scott Hodge, Lead Pastor, The Orchard Community
www.scotthodge.org

Dedication

*To the amazing people who call
Calvary Fellowship home.*

BOB FRANQUIZ

Contents

Things We Don't Speak of XIV

Leadership Strategies 1
    You're Always Communicating Vision 3
    How to Cast a Vision People Embrace 8
    Learn to See the Future 11
    Point A to Point B in Less Time 14
    It's All About Sunday! 19
    Momentum Doesn't Happen by Accident 25
    Create Start Times 29
    Focus on the Engine, not the Color 33
    Utilize Shortcuts 36
    Innovation Starts as an Expirment 40
    Frankenstein Churches 44
    The One and Only 48
    The Absence Factor 52
    The Best Teachers 56

Staffing Strategies 59
    Effective Hiring Practices 60
    You Only Hire Two Types of People 64
    Potential vs. Proven Performance 67
    Creative Staffing 71
    Tell Your Staff Where They Stand 75
    Giving People Rest 78

Let Your Wife Be Herself 81
The Leader who Gets to Carry a Guitar 84
The One Thing You Don't Want to do 89
Brick Layers and Bible Teachers 93
Create a Farm System 97
Ask! 102
Say "Thank You" 106

Ministry Strategies 110
Gauges on the Dashboard 111
Lessons in Outreach 116
The Big Ideas on Big Days 118
A New Way to Look at Your Community 122
Your Main Evangelistic Engine 125
How to Promote your Church 128
Money Matters 132
Make It Easy for People to Give 136
Supersizing Your Small Groups 140
Facility Matters 143
Barriers to Baptism 148
Membership Matters 152
The Lowdown on Follow-up 157
Eliminating "Bored" Meetings 161
Revisit Important Topics 165
How to Get Unstuck 169

Personal Development Strategies 173
Goal Setting 174

Effective Time 178
Management 178
The "Stop Doing" List 182
Learn to Delegate 185
From Whom Can You Learn the Most? 190
Get a Coach Help Yourself by Coaching Others 196
What Can a Senior Pastor Learn from a
Youth Pastor? 199
Create a Rhythm of Rest 202
How Leaders Refuel 206
Create Safeguards 210
Navigating Criticism 214
Don't Be Afraid to Challenge People 218
Church Hoppers 222
The World's Most Awkward Conversation 227
Ten Questions Leaders Should Ask Themselves 233
Keep Improving 238
Starbucks-Style Marketing to Your Community 243
The Tale of Two Karate Studios 246
Greenroom Pastors 249
How to Juggle while Preaching 252
Conference Syndrome 255

Leadership that Climbs Mountains 258
Endnotes 261

Foreword

Every once in a while, you meet someone who really stands out from the crowd, someone who has a sparkle in his eye—the kind of glimmer that tells you he is passionate about life and about his calling. The day I met Bob Franquiz, I knew I had met such an individual. Let me set the stage:

One of my greatest joys is training senior pastors from across the country. I love digging into the details of creating strong churches with other practitioners who are on the front lines every day. Each year, I have several hundred lead pastors come to me for training through my Senior Pastor Coaching Networks. I met Bob when he was accepted into one of these networks. In fact, he did so well in his first coaching network that he decided to join another—and then I handpicked him to participate in an Advanced Coaching Network with me. Bob's continual desire to absorb the principles and tools that could make him a better church leader inspired me, and I had a hunch that he would be able to inspire others, as well. That's why I asked Bob to become one of a handful of select, certified trainers for my ministry, Church Leader Insights. That unmistakable glimmer of passion I noted when I met Bob had proven to be just the tip of the iceberg.

Besides being a partner in ministry, Bob is a good friend. I am constantly impressed by his heart for leadership and for the healthy growth of the church. But, I do have to tell you, I have one very big disappointment with the book that you hold in your hands—I am disappointed that I didn't have access to it during the early years of my church, the Journey. The principles that Bob lays out in these pages would have helped me tremendously, as I am sure they will help you.

The novelist James Joyce once wrote, "Mistakes are the portals of discovery." Our mistakes cause us to see things in a new light; they cause us to grow if we view them through the right lens. The best thing about mistakes may be the fact that they don't have to be our own to be beneficial. If we are willing, we can learn as much from the mistakes of others as we can from the ones we make ourselves. We just have to view them as James Joyce did; we have to look at them, through them, and into them as the "portals of discovery" that they are.

In *Leadership Blurbs*, Bob opens up expansive portals of discovery for us. Thanks to his willingness to share what he has learned along the journey—or, more pointedly, his willingness to be candid about the mistakes he has made—you and I have an opportunity to multiply our own experience by his. While I am all for getting into the battle of church growth and making mistakes of your own, you would be unwise to dismiss the hard-learned lessons of those who have already traveled a similar path. Whenever you can, I encourage you to dissect the experience and missteps of others and take away every helpful principle you can find. Seek out leaders you admire, and ask them to tell you where the landmines have been on their path and how you can avoid them. Being open to wise counsel will lend to your exponential growth, both personally and professionally.

One of the most common barriers to church growth is a lack of intentional self-development on the part of the pastor. No organization can outgrow its leader. In fact, I've seen this problem time and time again in churches across the country. When a pastor stops growing personally, the sermons are stale, the passion for ministry wanes, the staff and volunteers fall into maintenance mode, and the church stops thriving. Two of the best ways to circumvent this growth barrier are 1) to read books that will stretch you and 2) to seek out mentors you admire.

With *Leadership Blurbs*, Bob has left you no excuse for shirking self-development. Not only is this a book that will challenge you, forcing you to think through the hard issues of day-to-day ministry, but it is written as if Bob were sitting across a table from you, sharing his heartfelt lessons in person. In the following pages, you will gain practical truth and teaching, yes, but you will also gain something you might not expect—a mentor to walk you through those truths and teachings one step at a time.

Here's my advice to you, church leader. Don't simply read this book. Use it. Write in the margins. Note the points that stand out to you. Discuss the lessons and their applications with your staff. Invite another church leader to lunch, and share what you are learning. Drink in this book. Memorize the mistakes that Bob has made, and combine them with your own. If you do, you will find exponential wisdom. And let me also challenge you: As you go forth in your ministry and in your life, follow the example set forth in these pages. That is, don't be stingy with what God teaches you. As you learn lessons and make mistakes of your own, turn them into portals of discovery for anyone willing to explore. God will use each of us to help the others on this path in unimaginable ways, as we are truly mindful of Paul's admonition to us in Hebrews:

"Let us consider how we may spur one another on toward love and good deeds...." (Hebrews 10:24).

Enjoy!

Nelson Searcy
Lead Pastor, The Journey Church (New York City)
Founder, www.ChurchLeaderInsights.com

Acknowledgements

This book would not have been written if it weren't for my friend Nelson Searcy. Nelson, thanks for investing in my life, so I could become a leader worth following.

Thanks to Mark Rodriguez and John Solaroli who serve as my assistant pastors at Calvary Fellowship. You guys make me want to be a better leader. Thanks for your friendship. I wouldn't want to do ministry with anyone else.

Thanks to the amazing people who call Calvary Fellowship home. I am honored to be your pastor.

Thanks to my amazing kids, Mia, Xander, and Olivia. I pray you grow up to see the Church be everything it can be.

Thanks to my wife Carey. You are the love of my life. Thanks for saying yes.

INTRODUCTION
Things We Don't Speak of

There's probably no worse feeling than realizing you've been seriously uninformed. Imagine the shock when the embattled Luke Skywalker heard those words from Darth Vader, "Luke…I am your Father!"

I can empathize with Luke because I know what it's like to go into battle and encounter astonishing discoveries that would have been great to know beforehand. I felt that way often in my first few years after planting a church in the fall of 2000. There seemed to be so much I was never told, so many apparent secrets withheld from me. I felt as if I was experiencing the wrath of the fine print I'd never taken time to read and now was facing the consequences.

In Bible college, I'd studied eschatology, soteriology, and the Bible's history and authenticity. I sat through studies of several books in the Bible and completed a survey of both testaments. I even had a class called Practical Christian Ministry in which I clocked hundreds of hours in the "sweatshop" of ministry.

Bible college led me to conclude that every issue was theological in nature, and the Bible had a verse for any problem or malady that would come my way. I memorized the verse my teachers quoted repeatedly: "His divine power has given to us all things that pertain to life and godliness" (2 Pet. 1:3).
But I was caught off guard by the onslaught of issues I faced as a church planter and senior pastor. I realized quickly there were many things with which the Bible doesn't deal.

Please understand. I believe the Bible is inspired and that it's all we need for daily living. And I'm forever grateful that gifted men of God, with a passion for His Word, and for young men like me who wanted to serve Him, instructed me.

But there are so many significant factors in church planting that the Bible doesn't directly address, and I wish someone would have sat down and told me about them. They don't pertain to salvation or the second coming, but they're still important if you're going to plant a church that succeeds.

To this end, I've written Leadership Blurbs. It's the result of countless conversations with church planters, senior and associate pastors, Bible college and seminary students, and others who want to see God's church succeed in the twenty-first century. Its purpose is to highlight the conversation topics that often don't make it to the platform at major Christian conferences, yet fill everyone's conversations during the breaks.

These practical issues in church planting and pastoring, plus the tensions they bring, can be like the forest-haunting creatures in M. N. Shyamalan's film The Village—they are "Those We Don't Speak Of." We know these issues exist; we just don't discuss them. The result is that many zealous men and women are much like the Jews of Paul's day, having "a zeal for God, but not according to knowledge" (Rom. 10:2).

My desire is to arm the people of God with some of the simple and not so simple things I've learned over the last seven years. Do I consider myself an expert in church planting or in pastoring a growing congregation? Hardly. Instead, I see myself as a fellow sojourner seeking to learn and grow in effectiveness for the God who saved me and called me into this most wonderful of vocations.

What you're about to read is truly the good, the bad, and the ugly of all I have and haven't done in the last seven years; my hope is that recognizing my successes and failures will help you as well.

So buckle up…because it's going to get bumpy.

PART I
Leadership Strategies

BOB FRANQUIZ

CHAPTER 1
You're Always Communicating Vision

In a recent conversation with a pastor, he asked, "How often do you communicate your vision to the church?" I responded, "Every week. And by the way, so do you." That response floored him, but I believe it to be the truth. Everything you do in your church communicates your vision. Pastors usually understand vision to be the mission of what God wants a particular local church to do. I agree with that definition; I would simply add that your vision is what's most important to you. Based on that definition, everything we do is communicating to people what's most important to us. In fact, if we were to look at three vital areas of your church, we could discern what is most important to you without reading a mission statement, hearing a compelling vision talk, or seeing a sign that speaks of your church's purpose.

Show Me the Money

The saying is true—money talks. If you want to know what is most important in your organization, look at your budget. Your budget is speaking volumes about the values of your church. My CPA likes to say that a profit-and-loss statement and balance sheet are painting a picture of a church. He says he doesn't even need to attend the church to know what the church is focused on, working towards, and values most. The same is true for your personal finances. If a person is spending 50 percent of his/her income on vacation, movies and candy, you can be sure that this person values entertainment above all else. Jesus said, "Where your treasure is, there your heart will be also" (Matt. 6:21).

You can say you bleed evangelism, but if all your budgeting dollars go towards meetings to get church people together, then your focus is fellowship, not evangelism. Your vision and your dollars should be headed in the same direction because wherever your resources are flowing is really your mission.

Show Me the Calendar

An entire wall in our offices at Calvary Fellowship is just a giant calendar of the current year. They have every event, meeting, series, staff vacation, national holiday, and school day off that matters to us as a church. What's interesting is when people visit our offices, they usually stop to look at this giant calendar to see what we're up to in the next few months. What amazes me is that you can tell what's important to us as a church just by looking at the calendar. You will see that we value planning, relevant expositional teaching, and maximizing each season to bring about the greatest evangelistic opportunities.

Your calendar is speaking as well. It might be communicating your desire to keep people busy every night of the week. It could be shouting a commitment to missions and evangelism. I spoke to a pastor, and he told me that one of his core values was to make sure his staff members were spending plenty of time with their families. I responded, "Then why do you have your church open every night of the week, knowing your staff will have to be here?" I didn't ask to be argumentative. I simply asked because his words and the calendar were speaking two different languages. No matter how brutal the facts, wise leaders listen to the words the calendar is speaking and make sure what they value most is reflected in the church's schedule.

Show Me the Motion

I was talking with a leader of a traditional church some time ago, and she showed me the newest mission statement they had crafted and framed to put on the wall of her church. It spoke of their commitment to evangelism, worshipping God, making disciples, and serving others. Each section of the mission statement was alliterated and well thought out. Yet what ran through my mind when I read this was that I would never have known that this church cared about any of these things because their actions spoke nothing of this. Actions do speak louder than words. Unfortunately, there's much more talking in the church these days than there is action. Sometimes, there's an unspoken mission. At the church I just mentioned, the unspoken mission is to care for those already in the church and pay no attention to those far from God. For others, the unspoken mission might be a desire for comfort, which overrides all other decisions for progress. Effective churches align their stated mission and unspoken mission. The unspoken mission simply reveals what others observe and who we really are. Our goal in our churches should be for the spoken and unspoken mission to match. It is here that a church reaches its full potential and becomes a masterful tool in God's hands.

A Vision Test

If you desire to know if your mission and reality are in alignment, I recommend you look over these three areas (money, calendar, and motion) and ask yourself the following questions:

- How much money did we spend this year directly on our spoken mission?

- When I am not directly communicating our vision, what are my words saying about what's important to me?

- If I couldn't speak, could people still know what's most important to us?

- If someone listened to me speak only once, would he/she know what our mission is?

- Does my personal calendar reflect what my mission is?

- Do we have an unspoken mission? Is it different from our spoken mission?

- How much of the church's resources are funding our mission or our unspoken mission?

- If my unspoken and spoken missions are out of alignment, what steps can I take to harmonize them?

Make no mistake—your mission is who you are as a church. Make sure that every voice in your church—your resources, your calendar, your actions, and your words—are saying the same thing. If you do, the resulting synergy, clarity and effectiveness will bring glory to God as you accomplish what God has called you to do.

BOB FRANQUIZ

CHAPTER 2
How to Cast a Vision People Embrace

As we mentioned in chapter one, you're always communicating vision. Yet there are times throughout the year when you must directly communicate a vision to take a bold step, begin a new initiative, or embrace a radical change. Many leaders have an amazing ability to pain a picture of the future, but people tend to have a difficult time filling in the gaps of how we get from here to there. Further still, people attend our churches because of the current state they are in, not dreaming of how things might change. The job of the leader is to cast a vision that people embrace by focusing on three key ingredients.

The Present Problem

In the book of Nehemiah, the walls of Jerusalem had been destroyed. Nehemiah arrives on the scene, reviews the situation, and then presents the current state of affairs to the inhabitants of Jerusalem. "You see the trouble we are in: Jerusalem lies in ruins, and its gates have been burned with fire" (Neh. 2:17a). Some might think this is an exercise in stating the obvious. I disagree. Before you can tell people about the glorious future you have planned, you have to create dissatisfaction with the status quo. You may laugh, but the masters of this are the late night infomercial people. They present the problem: for example, you're overweight. Then a doctor comes out and tells you all the health risks associated with carrying extra weight. What are they doing? They are causing every overweight person to feel the gravity of the present problem. Many preachers know how to do this. They bash people verbally for being sinners, and then the sermon ends without offering the tools to change or a vision of what a life of following God looks like. Nehemiah doesn't stop by sharing the problem, he moves on to the vision of the future.

The Proposed Solution

"Come, let us rebuild the wall of Jerusalem, and we will no longer be in disgrace" (Neh. 2:17b). Why would Nehemiah use the words "and we will no longer be a disgrace"? It is simply because Nehemiah wants to remind them of the past glory of Jerusalem under the reign of David, Solomon, and the other good kings of Judah. It's a picture of Jerusalem rightly representing God once again. Many pastors are gifted in communicating this aspect of vision casting. This is where we talk about how the facility is full, and we need to be sacrificial in our giving to build a facility where there is more space, so we don't turn anyone away who is seeking to know God. The point is that this is where you share the proposed solution to the problem. Unfortunately, this is where many leaders stop talking. Subsequently, this is why many leaders see limited results to their efforts. We have presented the problem and the solution, but we have neglected to share how to get to our desired result and why it needs to happen now.

The Potential Action

The last question a vision talk must answer is the question, "Why now?" There may be a problem, and you may have the solution, but if you don't create a sense of urgency, your vision won't gather much traction. Notice how Nehemiah did this: "I also told them about the gracious hand of my God upon me and what the king had said to me" (Neh. 2:18a). Nehemiah told them the story of how he went to a pagan king and told him about the walls of Jerusalem. Then this pagan king not only gave Nehemiah the time off, but he also gave Nehemiah the materials to rebuild the walls. Nehemiah is saying, "God has given us everything we need to do this. There is never going to be a better time to do this than right now!" These words ignited the hearts of the people of Jerusalem, and they responded in unison to do what Nehemiah proposed. "They replied, 'Let us start rebuilding.' So they began this good work" (Neh. 2:18b). What is the result? Success, buy-in, and the beginning of a great move of God in Jerusalem.

If you desire to lead your church through radical change and take on a bold vision, you need all three of these elements. Forget one, and your impact will be limited. Include them all, and you will build something great for God.

CHAPTER 3
Learn to See the Future

Leadership can be boiled down to one word—decisions. Leaders, by nature of their position, make many decisions each day. If you think through your day, my bet is you make dozens of decisions. I will even wager that many of these decisions range from big to small, from seemingly insignificant to earth shattering. That's the life of a leader. What I think about from time to time is what makes a leader a good decision maker? Certainly, there are intangible qualities such as spiritual maturity, discerAnment, and experience that all play into a leader's ability to make great choices. However, I also believe great leaders possess five qualities that make them extraordinary decision makers. Anyone can possess these qualities if they desire to be great leaders.

The Ability to Act Without 100 Percent Certainty

One of the myths of leadership is that one needs 100 percent of the facts before acting. The truth is that one almost never has 100 percent of the facts. If we wait until we have every piece of information before acting, every opportunity will pass us by. Great leaders know how much data they need before making a decision. Then, they are able to act with confidence.

The Ability to Listen to Others

Proverbs 11:14 says, "Where there is no counsel, the people fall; but in the multitude of counselors there is safety." Great leaders have great people around them who are willing to speak their minds. Many times leaders are caught up in the emotion of a decision, and it takes those around them to see another perspective. The leader who cannot listen to those around him will never aspire to greatness.

The Ability to Learn from Past Mistakes

Experience is a great teacher if we are willing to receive its counsel. I watch leaders make the same decision to justify a past mistake rather than learn from it. Resolve that the past is gone, and all we can do is learn from it. Some of the dumbest decisions I have made in my past have become some of my greatest counselors in my decision making in the present.

The Ability to Keep Fear in Check

Courage is not the absence of fear; it is moving ahead despite fear. The leader who says he has no fear is definitely lying. Instead, the skill here is to keep fear from paralyzing us. The fear that grips most leaders is the fear of failing. No one wants to fail. Yet every successful person knows that failure is part of success. It is common knowledge that the average millionaire has gone bankrupt twice in his lifetime. That being the case, what makes us think we will be any different and never experience failure? We will make the wrong choice at times. Yet the moment we let fear into the driver's seat, it's game over for us as leaders.

The Ability to Take Full Responsibility

Leaders don't have to be able to predict the future. They don't need to possess the gift of prophecy. They don't even need to be right every time they make a decision. The one thing they must do is take responsibility for their decisions. The leader who shifts blame and passes the buck will soon have no one following him because a leader must take responsibility. If you want to be right every time, don't be a leader; instead, be a critic. Critics are never wrong because they don't do anything. They simply watch everyone else live and take risks. Then, from their comfortable chair, they play the role of Monday morning quarterback and make their judgments. However, if you want to impact the future by creating it, you need to be a leader who assumes full responsibility for his actions and the actions of his organization.

CHAPTER 4
Point A to Point B in Less Time

"Someone once told me that time was a predator that stalked us all our lives. I rather believe that time is a companion who goes with us on the journey and reminds us to cherish every moment, because it will never come again."

—Captain Jean-Luc Picard (Star Trek Generations)

I have a friend who just got DSL. Can you believe it? In this day and age, a guy in his late twenties still using dial-up? Shocking to say the least! We live in a world that is continually getting faster. I recently sent my mom pictures of my daughter, and it took a whole two days to get to her. All I could think was, "Why didn't I just e-mail them, and they would have gotten to her in five minutes?" Here is where our problem lies. Everything in our lives happens so fast, that we expect our goals to be realized as quickly as Chef Boyardee can put warm raviolis on our plate. But for some reason, working towards our goals takes time, and if you're a leader, it's twice as long as you want it to be. So if God has called us to reach a city, start a ministry, or solve a problem, why is it taking so long for us to make progress? I mean if God is really in it, shouldn't it be easier?

Before I answer that, let me ask you another question. Have you ever seen a church just explode with growth immediately and another church that starts around the same time struggle in the beginning and slowly but surely gain momentum? Most of us have. So why do some seem to hit the ground running and others only to hit the ground? I believe it's because some leaders are more prepared, have clearer vision, and understand their communities better. Having said that, there's also a spiritual component that can't be quantified. There are some people and ministries that God chooses to bless for reasons that we will never know (Deut. 29:29). But I do know that we have the ability to maximize our talents (Matt. 25) and see the most fruit emerge from our lives if we will pay the price.

If you want to cut down the time it takes to get from point A to point B, you will have to devote yourself to three disciplines:

#1 — Learn everything you can from anyone you can

Rick Warren is famous for saying, "You can learn from anyone if you know the right questions to ask." The truth is that great leaders ask questions. The truly great leaders I have been around are genuinely curious people. They want to know how things work and how things can work better. They aren't interested in who gets the credit, nor are they interested in being original so much as they are in being effective. I go to Disney World about three times a year (one of the benefits of living in Florida), and I come home with dozens of ideas after every visit. I observe how they greet guests, direct guests, park guests, and seek to please guests, and it gives me ideas about how to interact with and serve people. I watch how they handle crowds, cars, and kids, and I gain insight into how I can better minister to people. So what can you learn from the guy who owns a successful pizza place down the street about serving people? I bet he could teach you at least 10 things, if you are looking to learn.

#2—Get around people who are ahead of you

Right now in your city, 10 people would love to spend an hour with you over lunch and tell you everything they know about ministry. Are you willing to call them? Let me be frank with you — pride and great leadership don't mix. Proud people don't reach new levels. Instead, they stay around a safe group of people where they will never be challenged or called out and told to grow up. If you are a pastor of a church of 250, you need to befriend a pastor that leads a church of 500. Find a pastor that is leading a church twice your size and ask him as many questions as you can think of that will help you go to the next level. What kinds of questions are those? Here's a sample:

How did your leadership style change between 250 and 500?
What was the biggest barrier to your growth at my stage?
How has a growing ministry impacted your family?
What were your key staff hires that helped you get to the next level?
What makes our city unique and what should I be aware of?

I meet with church planters regularly, and I can tell how they're going to fare within the first five minutes of our meeting. How do I know? By listening to the questions they ask or fail to ask. At times, a young pastor will sit in my office and tell me how great his church is and how backwards everyone else is. All the while, I'm sitting there listening, hoping he will ask me a question. Then after 55 (long) minutes, he'll say, "So tell me what you've learned that has helped you." My response is, "I'd love to, but we're out of time." Here's a lesson that I've learned: you're never learning when you're talking. We learn when we listen. How do you know when you're talking less than the person from whom you want to learn? When you're at lunch, you finish eating before they do. They're talking, so they can't chew! So, eat with one hand, and take notes with the other! The way to get from Point A to point B in less time is to learn from others. So make sure you're putting yourself in environments where you can learn from other leaders.

#3—Read as if there's no tomorrow!

The old saying is true, "Leaders are readers." If you aren't interested in reading, then you aren't interested in becoming a great leader. Think about this: would you like to sit with someone like John Maxwell and talk to him about leadership? I'm sure you would. I bet you wouldn't even say much. You would probably ask questions and let him talk until he was out of ideas. Do you know that John is available to meet with you for lunch today? Don't call his office and tell him I said he was expecting you. Instead, pick up one of John's books, buy a Whopper, and let John tell you everything he knows about leadership.

    I believe that leaders need to set time aside for reading everyday. It has been said that if you devote one hour to reading a day in a particular field, within five years, you will become a recognized expert in that field. Do you want to lead a great church? Read. Do you want to build a thriving student ministry? Read. Do you want to establish a world-class organization? Read! Reading is how you bridge the gap between lack of knowledge and wisdom. It's also how you get to your destination faster.

CHAPTER 5
It's All About Sunday!

Let me just come out and say it, Sunday is the most important day of the week for a church. The whole church comes together this day. The church hears instruction from God's Word, worships the Lord through singing, gives their offering, and the Gospel is preached to those who don't know Jesus on this day. Every Sunday is Super Bowl Sunday for the church! The Sunday services (or weekend services if you have Saturday night services) are also where you steer the ship as a leader.
The pulpit is the rudder, and it is from here that you set the direction, tone, and speed of your church. Other ministries are important and necessary, but none compare to the influence of those on Sunday.

So how do you emphasize Sunday over every other opportunity and ministry that calls to us for time, attention, and resources? Quite simply, it's by giving your best time, your best attention, and best resources to the Sunday services.

Giving Your Best Time to Sunday

Pastor, the first thing that you put on your schedule (and should not be moved unless it is a life or death emergency) is your study time. People will call with counseling needs, and staff will knock asking for "one minute" of your time, but we have to be disciplined enough to "Just say no" and give the appropriate amount of time to the study of God's Word to prepare for Sunday's message. Too often, I talk to pastors who are cramming to finish the message for Sunday because "stuff" got in the way. I can assure you that whatever came up, most of it is not more important than teaching God's truths to believers and preaching the Gospel to those who don't know Christ. Here's the reality: our study time isn't going to complain, it isn't going to write us a nasty e-mail if we neglect it, and it's not going to do something of which you never would have approved. If we don't use our study wisely and make appropriate time for study, we will walk into the pulpit unprepared. So make an appointment that you never break—an appointment with God to study His Word and be prepared to speak to God's people.

Giving Your Best Attention to Sunday

In their fantastic book, The Power of Full Engagement, Jim Loehr and Tony Schwartz write, "Energy, not time, is the fundamental currency of high performance."

For instance, my times of highest energy and greatest creativity are in the early morning. So, I get an early start on my study days to maximize my creative energy. Conversely, my times of lowest energy are in the mid-afternoon, so I schedule appointments during those times because listening doesn't require as much energy as creating. I encourage you to figure out what your best times are for study and preparation and block those out first. Then, schedule everything around your study time. It will increase your effectiveness exponentially as you cooperate with you body's natural rhythms.

Second, create moments where you give opportunity for feedback and evaluation of the Sunday service during the week. As a pastor, you must give your staff time to review the previous week's service, so you can improve in the areas that fell short. We do this in our weekly staff meetings. We set aside thirty minutes every week to discuss four questions about Sunday's services:

What went right?
What went wrong?
What was missing?
What was confusing?

We praise God for what went right. We send thank-you cards to show appreciation to volunteers who went beyond the call of duty. We encourage one another for a message well preached, a song well sung, or a video produced. We all need encouragement. This creates an opportunity to build up staff and servants who are working very hard.

Then we discuss the three other questions at the same time. This allows us to be specific about problems that took place on Sunday and how they can be remedied. Lastly, we assign the task of fixing the problem to a specific staff member. The solution may be as simple as buying duct tape (because doesn't that fix most problems anyway?) or cutting ten minutes off a future message (I believe duct tape could fix this problem too).

Giving Your Best Resources to Sunday

Your budget is speaking. It's telling you what you value most. If you buy many gadgets and pay your staff poorly, it's saying, "I care more about toys more than people." If you say you care about children's ministry but never invest resources into constantly improving it, you're saying, "Children don't really matter to me or my church." Looking at your budget will give you a good reference as to what's most important to you. If you want to make Sunday a priority in your budget, look at three areas that must be given the appropriate resources to excel. They are teaching, worship, and children's ministry.

Teaching Tools

Teaching is everything having to do with the communication of God's Word to the congregation. This means having the right books, software, and computer to do the job of studying. This also means investing in video if you want to communicate using that medium. It may mean buying something to give to people as they come in as an illustration for the message. It could mean a set design or prop that is going to drive the point of the message home. I believe you should spare no expense when it comes to the message. If spending that amount will increase the likelihood of life change, go for it!

Worship

Worship is not just singing, but also a life that's lived to the glory of God. But for the sake of our discussion, I will limit it to congregational singing in the Sunday service. Too many churches I walk into have speakers that are blown and making awful noises while the basketball court was just repaved! I was in a church recently where half the lighting didn't work in the sanctuary, but they had just purchased brand new appliances for their kitchen. Call me Fred Sanford, but I nearly had a heart attack right on the spot! If we learn anything from the Tabernacle in the wilderness, it's that God was very interested in creating an experience when His people came to worship Him. I believe we must do the same in our worship experiences. Does the band have the right equipment? Are there enough speakers to fill the room? Is the video gear totally outdated and difficult to use? Is there enough lighting to create the mood you want? A first-time guest will spend more time in your sanctuary than in any other area. What is this area communicating to them?

Kids are People Too

Children's ministry is the one place where you don't want to skimp! Go all out in your children's ministry, and make due in other areas. The most important thing to a parent is their kids, so show them you believe that, too, by creating an incredible environment for kids. You need to communicate this value to parents in three ways:

1. Safety. Disney World's number one value in their theme parks is safety. Why? Because they understand that the most important element to gaining trust comes through the parents knowing their child is safe. Parents will have a hard time leaving their kids in a hallway that you've "converted" into a classroom. Look at your children's ministry through the eyes of a guest. You wouldn't leave your kids in a hallway with two disinterested teenagers and neither will they. Make providing the safest possible environment for children your primary goal.
2. Cleanliness. Parents are concerned about the environments their kids are in. They want these spaces to not only be safe, but also clean. If you are in a portable facility, work extra hard to make sure that school, community center, or theater are spotless in your children's areas.
3. God's Love. Parents are expecting you to do this. Prove you can provide a safe, clean space for their kids, and they will trust you to teach their kids the Bible.

However you slice it, Sunday is the most important day of the week. It's the day you interact with the most people that are connected to your church and all the guests they brought with them. So, put your best foot forward by keeping Sunday first in your mind, your resource allocation, and in your planning.

CHAPTER 6
Momentum Doesn't Happen by Accident

When I was in California in 2005, I had an experience that I'd never want to relive. My wife and I were driving from Los Angeles to Newport Beach, and I never checked the gas tank. As Murphy's Law would have it, I felt the car decelerating, and even though I floored the pedal, nothing happened. Then I looked at the gas tank and noticed the needle was about an inch below "E" (whoops!). I saw an exit and immediately took it, coasting on my previous speed. Have I mentioned that during this entire episode, my wife was asleep?

I pulled off the highway, and as I went down a hill, I gained speed. The lights at the bottom of the hill turned green just in time, as I thanked God and made a hard left. I saw a gas station to the right, but I had to make another turn. I made the turn, but the gas station was at the top of a hill, and slowly, my car came to a halt.

I woke my wife up and told her to take the wheel while I got out and pushed. If you've ever had to push a car that's run out of gas, you know what kind of humiliating experience it is. Little children point in your direction and say, "Mommy, why is that man outside of his car? Daddy, why is his face so red that it looks like it's going to explode?" It wasn't my best moment. Then, two guys ran out into the middle of the street from the Honda dealership and helped me push the car to the gas station located on the corner. To this day, I believe those two men were angels disguised as car salesmen (no one would ever suspect car salesmen as being connected to God at all— just kidding!).

I used to tell that story and say, "My momentum (and a couple of guys) pushed me to the gas station. But that's not true. Momentum isn't the same as coasting. Coasting implies deceleration. Momentum, on the other hand, implies acceleration and achievement. Momentum is when I'm approaching a hill, and my former speed and current acceleration lead to getting over steep terrain. The same is true for churches. Churches that learn to build and navigate momentum experience tremendous results. The question we should ask is, "How does a church gain and sustain momentum? We will discuss four ways.

1. *The leader is constantly growing.* This is going to be a theme throughout this book. If you're not engaged in growing your leadership, you're not engaged in leadership because at its core, leadership implies growth and change. Every leader has to look at himself soberly and see the areas where he must

continue growing. The leader who isn't growing will quickly kill any momentum the church has through bad decisions and poor communication.

2. *The church is "winning." Everyone wants to win.* No one signs on to set up deck chairs on the Titanic. Churches that never stop building momentum are churches that celebrate when the mission of the church is being fulfilled. Whatever your mission statement might be, I'm sure it's a variation of the wording in the Great Commission. So, when people come to know Jesus as their Savior, celebrate that. When people are baptized, celebrate that. When new members are added to the church, celebrate that. The point is that momentum is built when people see the ball being pushed up the field.

3. *New believers are added.* Brand new Christians are the greatest evangelists on the planet. Why? No one they know is yet a follower of Jesus, and they can't wait to tell their friends what they have just experienced. If you want to have a church that's exploding with excitement and momentum, make sure you have plenty of young Christians in your midst.

4. *Anticipation is building.* "Leadership is anticipation," according to Steve Stroope, Senior Pastor of Lake Pointe Church in Rockwall, Texas. It's the art of leading people to what's next. Anticipation builds momentum in the hearts of people. People love knowing there's something happening next and that the best is yet to come.

You have two options: either gain and sustain momentum or get out and push. Let me spare you the pain of the latter and say that it takes ten times the work to get out and push, and you don't get nearly the same level of results. Momentum on the other hand is also hard work, but it's a much smoother ride.

CHAPTER 7
Create Start Times

One of the most faithful friends for church leaders is start times. People have an easier time getting involved in something when it is beginning than diving into the middle. I first learned this lesson when I was running a Bible college. I found that the campuses of our school, which worked on a semester system, had a lower attendance than those who worked from a quarterly system. The key was that the semester campuses had three start times, and the quarter system campuses had four start times. The lesson is that the more opportunities you give for people to start at the same time as everyone else, the more likely you are to reach more people.

I have found this to be a key component for building momentum. You gain natural momentum every time you use the word "new" or "starting." Movie companies hype up opening days to build momentum for a film and put all their energies into advertising for that day. Madison Avenue advertisers understand this principle as well. Just walk through the aisles of your local grocery store, and you'll be hard pressed to find a product that doesn't have an adjective of "new" or "improved" to describe its brand.

As I mentioned in my college experience, start times improve attendance and involvement. People naturally respond to something when it is first starting. It's the science behind the "Grand Opening" sign or the "Under New Management" banner in front of a restaurant. People respond to something when it is new, or a significant enough change warrants another look.

Another reason start times are helpful is because they give everyone the feeling they are on equal footing. Walking into a small group the first week isn't intimidating when it is the first week for everyone in the group. I can assure you that breaking into a group that's been together for two years is not as easy. The anxiety factor goes up, and the chances of that new person showing up again go down dramatically.

I love start times because they give the church a reason to build excitement. It's one thing to be teaching a message as part of your Ephesians series. It's quite another thing to say, "We're going to be starting a brand new series of studies on the subject of marriage and family as we continue to explore the book of Ephesians. We are going to be talking about issues that are relevant to your family and those to whom you're close. Here are six invite cards for you to give to your family and friends who you think would benefit from a series like this one." This puts the church in a place of excitement and expectancy that came through planning a start time behind which the church can rally.

So what are natural start times that churches can capitalize on? Here are five:

1. *The calendar.* January 1 is a day on which everyone wants a fresh start. Why not teach a message or series of messages on how this year can be different? In January, people are thinking about newness, learning, and change, so start a series through a book of the Bible and capitalize on that.
2. *Easter.* This is a time when many new people are coming to Christ. It's also your highest attended Sunday of the year. This is a great time to begin a series of teachings that draws people into the life of your church. I normally do not teach a stand-alone Easter message. Rather, Easter is usually part one of a series of studies. This way, the newcomer has attended on a start day and is more likely to stay.
3. *Teaching series.* While mentioned indirectly in the first two suggestions, throughout the year, build into your preaching certain times where you are beginning something new that can catalyze your congregation and turn them into an inviting army. This will also give your irregular attendees an opportunity to come to church and I hope be more committed.
4. *Small groups.* Our church has seen tremendous success in seeing those in our congregation get into small groups. I believe the major reason for this has been the implementation of a semester-based small-group system. The natural starting and ending of groups several times

throughout the year invites the addition of new group members more than in any other small group model I have ever seen.

5. *Change in leadership.* Whenever there is a significant change in leadership in a church, such as a new senior pastor or worship leader, there can be significant momentum by letting people know of the change. Even if someone wasn't too keen on the church in the past, a change of this magnitude can totally change the flavor of the church and attract those who previously didn't attend.

CHAPTER 8
Focus on the Engine, not the Color

I love The Brady Bunch. I watched the show growing up with a religious devotion. One episode describes the methods of many churches. Greg Brady gets his driver's license and buys a car for $100. The car doesn't run. Speaking of how bad the car sounds, Mike Brady (Greg's dad) says, "Sounds like a flock of geese heading south!" So, what does Greg do to fix the problem? He paints the car black! Sure enough, the car still doesn't run, and he ends up junking the car at the end of the episode. This is what happens in many churches. If things aren't going well, we "change the color" and change something cosmetically about the church while never really getting to the real problem, which lies under the hood.

A couple of years ago, I went to a conference and sat through two days worth of sessions on creatively titling your sermon series, branding your messages, and using catchy phrases in your marketing. Let me say, I have no problem with these things.

My issue is, if the problem standing between most churches reaching their communities was idioms and invites, I think everyone would have been reached by now. Unfortunately, the challenges aren't cosmetic; they're systemic.

We think that a new Web site, a new sign, or a painted building is the key to continued growth. While none of these things are bad in and of themselves (in fact, I'd recommend you do all of these things), they aren't the primary reasons why God blesses a church and how barriers to growth are overcome. Instead, the "engine," or systems of your church, is the area where you need to devote the bulk of your time. Most conferences and books focus on the color of the car, that is, the external things involved in church. My problem is, these usually aren't the major issues that are keeping a church from reaching its full redemptive potential.

Churches that want to reach their cities are going to have to ask hard questions, such as Are our methods of evangelism reaching people? Is our system to disciple people producing fully devoted followers of Jesus? Is our worship service geared exclusively for the mature believer, or can a person seeking to know Jesus find Him through an understandable message and engaging music? Is our current staff equipped to take this church to the next level? Do we really love lost people more than we love our own preferences? This is much more than simply adding a button on our Web site. It's restructuring what we do for fulfilling the Great Commission.

Why don't we look under the hood and deal with the problems? Here's the honest answer: because it's messy, and most of us (me included) want to be liked. And when I start messing with the systems of the church, this is where real change comes from, and to get to these systems is sometimes a war. Here's how I've learned to deal with the fear of not wanting to get under the hood. I call it the "Tom principle." A pastor on my staff and I have a mutual friend named Tom. We went to Bible college together, and he pastors a church in another state. One day, we needed to make a hard decision that neither of us wanted to make. It was a "get under the hood and get yourself dirty" kind of decision, but we were wrestling with it. We wanted to paint the hood and say we did what God wanted us to do. So, I picked up the phone and said, "Let's call Tom, and tell him everything we know. With no emotional attachment and no fear, what will Tom tell us to do?"

I put the phone down, and we both knew what had to be done. We had to get under the hood and do what leaders do—focus on the engine, not the color of the car and get our hands dirty. Focusing on what brings results isn't fun or easy, but it's what great leaders do.

CHAPTER 9
Utilize Shortcuts

"These things happened to them as examples and were written down as warnings for us, on whom the fulfillment of the ages has come. So, if you think you are standing firm, be careful that you don't fall!"

—1 Cor. 10:11–12

Leading 2.5 million people had to be challenging, to say the least. In fact, the books of Exodus, Leviticus, Numbers, and Deuteronomy are packed full of stories ranging from the miraculous to the tragic. Yet, the Apostle Paul, while recounting some of the most famous stories in the Old Testament tells the church at Corinth that all of these stories are there for us as examples. It's been said that experience is the best teacher. I believe there's an even better teacher: the experiences of others. The truth is, none of us has enough time to make all of our own mistakes. We need to learn from the successes and failures of others, so we can reach our goals faster. Yet, learning from the experiences of others is a learned ability. I believe it takes mastering three skills that we will discuss.

You Can Learn from Any Experience

When I was just starting out in ministry, I was lamenting to a mentor about a supervisor I had. He was a terrible manager, and I was frustrated because I was looking to work for someone I could learn from, as I knew I would plant a church someday. This mentor told me that every time this manager made a poor decision, he was teaching me. He told me that I could learn from any experience; I just had to learn to extract the principles. Too many times, we're looking for the answers to come easily. In real life, the answers come to us in the form of questions, sad stories, and a host of other unconventional means.

Business philosopher Jim Rohn once said, "You can learn just as much from failures as you can from successes. The problem is, the guys who have failed don't usually give seminars." The moral is that every story or experience is an opportunity for us to learn important lessons that can keep us from making poor choices or missing out on an important opportunity.

Ask Questions

My pet peeve, when a church planter or pastor has called my office to make an appointment to meet with me, is he arrives without pen, paper, or questions in hand. Some are quite honestly, completely unprepared. It's almost as though they expect something magical to happen in our meeting that they will never forget. Brian Tracy was right when he said, "You are not learning anything when you are talking." I encourage leaders to ask questions if they really want to learn.

When I make an appointment with a leader I want to learn from, I prepare for the meeting. I write out a list of questions I want to ask (usually more than I will be able to ask in a thirty- to sixty-minute meeting). I keep follow-up questions in mind based on their answers. I bring a notebook and pen, so I can write down the answers to their questions because the old saying is true that the shortest pencil is better than the longest memory. If I go out to lunch with a leader I want to learn from, I never order anything messy (like chicken wings). I order something easy to eat, so I can eat quickly and keep writing and asking questions. My goal in meetings like this is to say as little as possible, so the person I'm meeting with can say as much as possible.

What Key Decisions Were Made

Some of the most important things to know about a leader's journey are the major decisions they've had to make during their years of leadership. I like to ask leaders about their church's history. If a leader I'm meeting with is leading a church that went through a period of tremendous growth, I like to ask what happened during that time that may have contributed to the church's growth. Many times, great insight can be gained. For instance, the church of one leader I met with doubled in size over the course of a year. When I asked him about this, he immediately pointed me to key areas in his church that he staffed just before the growth. Sometimes, moving the church's location was the catalyst; other times, it was the hiring of a teaching pastor or the development of an area of ministry. Whatever it was, it's important to ask what key decisions led to the church's move to the next level.

Yes, experience is the best teacher. But it doesn't have to be your experience that teaches you. Learn from the experiences of others, and you will put yourself on the track to getting farther faster.

CHAPTER 10
Innovation Starts as an Expirment

Thomas Edison is quoted as saying, "I have not failed. I've just found 10,000 ways that won't work."[iv] This is an important attitude in ministry because if we are afraid to experiment and fail, we will never be innovative and take our ministries to the places they need to go.

Experimentation is part of how we learn what's most effective in our context. For example, how do you know what are the best times to have Sunday services at your church? You have to experiment with different times and see what's best. We have changed our service dozens of times over the years, and we aren't done changing them. As we add services, we're constantly trying to discern what the most effective times are and how much time between services is ideal. I recognize that's an easy example. How about starting a ministry or campus or planting a new church? Is there a higher level of risk involved?

Absolutely. We must do our due diligence in getting all the data we can to see if this venture is viable and has a strong chance of succeeding. Yet, at some point, there are no more facts to look at, no more strategy meetings to attend, and no more conversations to have with other leaders. There comes a moment when the appropriate response is action.

So what is keeping you from trying something new? I have found three major blocks that keep leaders from experimenting and discovering some new process, system, or venture:

What Will Other Leaders Think

The Bible says, "Fearing people is a dangerous trap, but trusting the Lord means safety" (Prov. 29:25). There's nothing wrong with fear; it's a normal emotion. Yet, it's whom I fear that causes me trouble. When I fear God and realize that I cannot please God without faith, it propels me to trust God more and step out in faith. When I fear people, God becomes very small in my life, and people become enormous. Truth be told, other leaders are dying to find out if something new will work. Many of them won't try anything new because they have not been able to overcome this block.

Can you imagine what the Church would look like if people took a chance and risked the status quo for more effectiveness for the kingdom of God? I know what it would look like. It would look like the book of Acts. In the early church, people traded control for greater effectiveness. People exchanged fear for faithful service. Believers exchanged passivity for boldness. Disciples gave up comfort for converts. Did they receive criticism? Yes, but what's interesting is the criticism they received was from those who wanted to experience the same thing but were unwilling to risk anything.

Loss of Control

There is a feeling of being out of control when you step out into something new and experiment. The downside is that you don't know what the outcome will be. I ask myself this question all the time: Am I willing to live with what I have now by not acting? If I don't change something, nothing will change. If I try something new, at least I have the possibility that things could turn around. I've found there's an interesting dynamic in regards to people who refuse to try something new and change their lives. There's a staff member who is grossly unhappy in his ministry position. He complains, has a rotten attitude, and hasn't smiled in years. The best thing for this person is to leave his current position and move on to another ministry. Yet, he refuses to leave. Why does this happen? It happens because many times we would rather be unhappy in the misery we know, rather than venture out and face the possibility of experiencing a different type of misery. Even though there is so much upside to leaving and far less risk, many will stay because the loss of the familiar is too much to bear.

"If I Fail, People Will Think I'm a Bad Leader"

Honesty alert: This phrase stalks me. It's true that if you continually make bad choices, people will stop following you. Yet, if you show a pattern of consistency in your life, people will not label you a poor leader for making a wrong turn now and then. People who fail when they step out into the unknown aren't bad leaders; they are simply leaders. People who won't step out and lead have nothing to risk and, conversely, nothing to gain. I cannot be a leader without venturing out and taking risks. If I fail, then it was simply a learning experience.

The benefits of trying new and better ways of doing things have too much potential to allow fear to keep us on the sidelines. The guys on the field are the only ones who take the hits, but they are also the only ones who score touchdowns.

CHAPTER 11
Frankenstein Churches

I honestly can't keep up anymore with the many types of churches. There are traditional churches, new paradigm churches, emerging churches, purpose-driven churches, Bible churches, house churches, cell churches, mega-churches, multi-site churches, denominational churches, non-denominational churches, and inter-denominational churches, to name a few. But another type of church doesn't too get much press but is in every city I know— Frankenstein churches.

These churches are built piece by piece without a clear vision in mind. The leader and staff go to a conference, hear a compelling talk or read an inspiring book, and, as a result, add another piece to the organization without considering its impact on the church as a whole. Most churches don't start out as Frankensteins. Instead, they start out simple and full of possibility. Then, someone gets an idea to add a ministry or program. Someone needs to sit down at this moment and think long and hard before saying yes, but more often than not, it doesn't happen. A piece is added to the church. Then another. Then another. Next thing you know, the simple church you once knew has been morphed into a monster that's terrorizing the villagers.

Every one of us falls into one of two groups. Either we are in an organization that has a clear mission and simple structure, or we're in a church where the mission is cloudy and the structure is more complicated than the story line on All My Children. I have been in both camps while in the same church. I feel as though we went on a roller coaster ride. We started simple, got complicated, and then got simple again. So, let me share with you how to get simple and stay simple:

1. *Ask the question, "Does adding _____ help us accomplish our mission?"* This might sound like an easy question to answer, but it's not. We added ministries based on, "Well, it isn't harming us or hindering us from accomplishing our mission." Unfortunately, we were kidding ourselves because we were unaware that sideways energy hurts an organization almost as much as negative energy. Sideways energy is the time, money, resources, and momentum wasted on endeavors that don't get you closer to your goal. So, "it's not hurting anyone" isn't a good enough answer. If it requires someone's oversight, effort, and attention, and it's not pushing the ball up the field in regards to the mission given to you by God, then it is hurting the

cause, and you must be courageous enough to say "no."

2. *Kill what isn't working.* This seems so obvious, but it takes a man with a stomach of steel to do it. When I stood up in front of our church and told them we were canceling our midweek service in favor of small groups, I thought I was going to throw up! Was our midweek service full? No. Was it half full? No. Yet, it was painfully difficult to end. There were feelings of failure and expectations that were unfulfilled. It was not an easy decision. Yet as I type this four years after making this tough leadership decision, I know it was the right thing to do. When we moved our men's, women's, and singles ministries into small groups because the previous format simply wasn't getting the results we hoped, it ruffled a few feathers, but it was the right call to make. Having said that, please don't underestimate the inner fortitude it will take to make these types of choices. However, I can promise that you will look back with joy after making the right decision.

3. *Focus all your energy on what brings results.* At Calvary Fellowship, we do four things: Sunday service, children's ministry, youth ministry, and small groups. We may add something else to that list in the future, but it's going to take more than a good idea to get on that exclusive list. Because of our laser focus, we staff, budget, and give attention to these areas and are able to do them with excellence. Too many times, we try to be a jack-of-all-trades in our churches (a major cause of the Frankenstein syndrome) and wind up doing nothing well. Before you even think about branching out, make sure your church is hitting home runs

every weekend in the worship service and with children's and student ministries. Get above average results in your small groups, and then, if there's time in people's schedules, money left in the budget, and a need (many times if you do the basics well, the need for extraneous ministries goes away), then prayerfully consider it.

It's much easier to add another bolt to Frankenstein's head or attach another limb than it is to remove one (just ask Dr. Frankenstein). That's why we must be ever so careful when we add items to the church's agenda—because cutting it may be more painful than you realize.

Check this out!
FREE RESOURCES
geared towards helping you grow as a leader, visit
www.NINJAarchive.com

CHAPTER 12
The One and Only

"There can be only one."
—*Connor McLeod (Highlander)*

When it comes to who drives the car that is your church, there can be only one person—the senior pastor. Many can give input, some can offer alternatives, a few can be a sounding board, but in the end, there can be only one leader. This topic of who really runs the church might be the one that comes up the most when I talk to existing church leaders. The reason? The senior pastor has a God-given vision he is seeking to implement and hands are coming out of nowhere to grab hold of the wheel, thus rendering the vision of the senior pastor impotent. How did this happen?

It all started when the church began. A group of people loved each other and believed in the calling that God placed on a man to start a church. Everyone was friends, everyone had a voice, and everyone was happy. Then, God began to bless the church, and it wasn't just five people in a living room anymore. It was one hundred people meeting in a rented facility.

One day, the pastor had to make a decision and couldn't inform everyone. Here is where the problem started. The person who wasn't informed didn't like the decision and began to think that the pastor had too much authority. So, to ensure that he would never get left out of the loop, he said, "Let's form a committee to talk about such issues." It seemed reasonable enough. I mean, who doesn't want more input? But what many leaders learn is that committees aren't about input; they are about control. They are cloaked in many other names, but these groups exist to make sure that nothing changes without this group's approval. The church soon begins to stall and stagnate, and eventually, the vision God gave to the senior pastor becomes lost in the minutes of a committee meeting. What happened? Here's a better question: how can you make sure this never happens to you?

Here's the principle: God always gives leadership to a person, not a committee. People may not have liked Moses, but they knew God had put him in charge. The same could be said for Joshua, David, Solomon, Nehemiah, and the pastor of every New Testament church in the book of Acts. I believe that the senior pastor needs to set up a structure that allows the staff and him to lead the church without unnecessary red tape. But what about accountability? My answer is, "What about it?" If a leader isn't accountable to God, he isn't going to be accountable to any group. Also, there seems to be a tendency in churches to believe that without someone watching over the pastor's shoulder, he will go crazy and steal money from the church or make unwise decisions for the church.

My philosophy is that the one who took the greatest risk in following God's leading should have the right to lead. If a pastor is willing to put his life on the line, uproot his family, and live in financial uncertainty while the church is starting, he should have the right to lead. I believe leading a church is much like driving a car. That being the case, you can't have more than one driver at any given time.

So, here's what I propose to every church leader and every person following a man of God:

Operate from a position of trust. Believe the best in your pastor. He has made many sacrifices that you will never know to serve God in the ministry. Honor that, and respect it. This isn't to say that the senior pastor is infallible. My point is, instead of operating from a place of suspicion, begin from a place of trust, believing that the pastor is serving the best interests of the church.

Have accountability. I don't know of one pastor who is seeking to honor God with his life that doesn't seek the very best counsel. The question is, "Who is the best counselor for a pastor?" I believe it is another pastor. A fellow senior pastor that has been faithfully serving his congregation is the best person to counsel another pastor. This is why I recommend that pastors should add other senior pastor, and not members of their congregation, to the church's board of directors. The reasons are endless, but when it comes to issues of staffing, compensation, building facilities, and church governance, a seasoned pastor has been there, whereas even the most faithful church member probably has not. I'm sure there are exceptions to this, but keep in mind, they are exceptions.

Does this set up the senior pastor as a dictator? Absolutely not! Moses was clearly the leader as the children of Israel traveled across the desert, but he was not a dictator. In fact, Hebrews 3 speaks of Moses as a servant. The reality is that a committee won't turn a pastor into a servant if he isn't one already. Only the Spirit of God can do that. The only thing the imposed rule of a committee will turn a pastor into is a hireling. Yet, Jesus told us that a good shepherd lays his life down for the sheep (John 10). The pastor who wants to lead his church is not trying to be a dictator; he is seeking to be a shepherd in the fullest sense of the word. Do you know what happens when a church allows a pastor to take the wheel and drive? Great things! The church goes to the place that God intended!

CHAPTER 13
The Absence Factor

The true test of leadership is not what happens when you are present. I believe the true test of leadership is what happens in your organization when you aren't there. Great leaders do more than just inspire the troops. They create systems that are reproducible, develop a structure that is not completely dependent on one person, and they hire the best staff possible who can function without the need for constant supervision. I want to work through these three issues because I believe that with these areas operating on all eight cylinders, it will create the kind of church, which never stops growing and reaching people.

The Right Systems

What difference can effective and reproducible systems make? All the difference in the world. The most famous illustration of this is McDonald's. The McDonald brothers had a great idea, but when they started to expand their horizons and open new stores, they could not sustain the growth, and they floundered. It was only when Ray Kroc saw the potential in franchising the McDonald's brand that a burger-making empire was born. How did he accomplish this? By creating systems. Think about it: McDonald's has the ability to take fifteen-year-old kids who won't clean their room and train them to make the same sandwich all over the world. This isn't magic. Instead, a series of systems they have developed has been reduced to their least common denominator.

What could this mean for your church? What if you took areas of ministry in your church and created a system anyone could reproduce? It would take your ministry to the next level. If you had a detailed follow-up process for newcomers that could be followed step by step, you could have just about anyone serving in that area and know you were going to get the same result. Think through every area of service in your church—how much easier and effective would ministry be if you could systematize positions in such a way that expectations and duties were clear and measurable?

The Right Staff

I like to say, "Hire Type 'A' people or you will 'B' frustrated." We don't hire people that need to be motivated or need constant supervision. A staff member who can't organize his or her time or tasks isn't going to cut it in our organization. I hope the same is true for yours. Too many pastors spend their time managing people who can't manage themselves rather than engaging in the activities that will take the church where it needs to go. Before entering ministry, I worked for a company who manufactured home accessories. A girl on our staff couldn't seem to get her work done, so the CEO decided to spend thirty minutes every morning creating a to do list for her so she could stay on track. I was a young college student at the time, and even I knew that was a waste of time for a CEO. Instead of accepting that this person wasn't fit for the position she was in, he wasted valuable time that could have been spent leading his company into the future.

The right type of staff doesn't need a boss to organize their day. Quality staffs need knowledge of the mission, a clear understanding of the goal, and the space to get the job done. The right staff will take a load off the senior pastor and will manage themselves. God will only bless a church to the degree that the staff can handle the blessing. So, if you want to lead a church that reaches thousands with the Gospel, one of the factors to reaching that goal is a staff that can lead themselves and others.

The Right Structure

Too many organizations operate based on a structure that limits growth and strips leaders of their leadership. If the only decision maker in the church is the senior pastor, nothing can be done when the pastor isn't around. However, if authority is dispensed with responsibility, then decisions can be made at each level of the organization. Rick Warren is famous for saying, "You can structure your church for control or growth, but not both." Too many senior leaders want total control and yet are dumbfounded when their church never reaches many people. To structure a church for growth means there are decisions in which the senior pastor isn't involved. While there is always accountability, an underlying level of trust permeates the organization. When an atmosphere of trust is alive in a church, there is a freedom where even if you aren't there, the best decision is being made.

CHAPTER 14
The Best Teachers

One of the things I see too often in the church world is young pastors going to big church conferences to learn from the "Big Dogs" about what's hot in the church. Well-intentioned mega-church pastors stand up and share what they are doing this year to reach out, what latest series has attracted new people, or what key staff member has helped them overcome a personal barrier in their church. Here's the problem—it's not that helpful, unless you have a church that's similar in size!

When you have two people on staff, hearing about a new department that just was added to a staff of 200 isn't going to help you push the ball down the field. I have learned that the people who can help us the most are those who are one or two steps ahead of us. If you are leading a church of 100, find a pastor of a church of 200–300 that has a similar style to yours, and you will find that an hour lunch with the pastor is infinitely more helpful that flying cross-country to hear about what a church of 20,000 is doing. I think a good rule of thumb is to look for a church that's at least 50 percent larger than your church. If you're leading a church of 500, a church running 750–1,000 in attendance can save you many mistakes if you're willing to take notes and take heed to what is being shared.

What are the key questions to ask a pastor who is leading a church that's larger than yours is? I believe there are ten vital questions to ask. I ask these questions every time I'm around a leader who's a little further down the road than me:

1. What is the biggest change you've seen in your life since your church has grown?
2. What was the most strategic staff hire that helped you get to the next level?
3. How has your church changed from X number of people (where you are) to today (where he is)?
4. How has your leadership changed in this last season of ministry?
5. What books have helped you to get to the stage you are in?
6. What are the pitfalls I need to look out for in my stage of ministry? (Remember, he's already been there.)
7. How have you had to guard your time differently?
8. How has your interaction with staff, volunteers, and the church at large changed?
9. Has your schedule changed at all?
10. Is there anything I haven't asked that is important for me to know? (Remember, no matter how much we prepare, we

always have blind spots. This question becomes a catchall of sorts where he can share something that might be in his heart.)

11. Do you read my blog? (Just kidding! Bad question.)

Here's the key—if you can get around people who have been where you are recently ("recently" being the operative word), you can glean incredible wisdom that will help you immediately in your current situation.

PART TWO:
Staffing Strategies

CHAPTER 15
Effective Hiring Practices

What will make or break your church is deciding who will be the people that lead and represent the organization—the staff. I have made so many hiring mistakes that I could fill several chapters with dos and don'ts. Yet the key to learning is not to repeat the same mistakes but learn from them. So, I decided to become an expert on hiring. I read everything I could on hiring, and every time I had a chance to talk with a leader, I would ask him about his hiring practices. What I learned was that five critical areas must be considered if you and I are going to choose well.

Look from Within First

I am a firm believer that your next staff member is more than likely already in your church. He or she is probably serving faithfully in an area of ministry and making an impact through his or her influence. I am happy to say that nearly 100 percent of our staff hires have been from within, and I don't regret it for a moment. Are there situations where you hire from within, it doesn't work out, and it gets a little messy? Yes, but I'd rather risk that than bring in a stranger any day. People inside your church already believe in the vision and mission of the church. So, adding them to your staff brings with it fewer surprises.

Obey the Rule of Three

Brian Tracy in his book, Hire and Keep the Best People, talks about what he calls "the rule of three." His principle is that you interview someone three times, in three different places, and three different people should interview them. The purpose of this is to identify if this person is right for your organization. You can learn quite a bit about a person based on how they treat a server in a restaurant when you're interviewing them or how he interacts with his wife in an office setting.

Testing...Testing...

I am a big fan of testing potential staff members through the tools that are available to us. Two tests that have been very effective for us are Gallup's Strengthfinder and the Myers-Briggs Assessment. We don't hire anyone without the candidate taking those tests. I have also found that these tests help the individual learn quite a bit about himself or herself. I recently sat with a person I was interviewing, and I told him this position wasn't a great fit for him. They understood and were thankful for the interview process because they learned so much about themselves through the testing process.

The Three C's

Bill Hybels made the three C's famous in his book Courageous Leadership. His rule is that when hiring, he is looking for character, competence, and chemistry. The staff members you hire and serve with need to have all three if you're going to build a world-class staff that will take your church to the next level. Character is a non-negotiable quality that trumps all the others. (See chapter seventeen for more on character). Competence is expertise in their position. The reputation non-profit organizations have is that they have nice people working in them, but most of them are incompetent. The Bible says, "Sing to him a new song; play skillfully, and shout for joy" (Ps. 33:3). This doesn't just apply to musicians. It applies to every area of the church. Excellence honors God and inspires people, so we need to put people in areas where they are competent and skilled. Lastly, chemistry is feeling they fit in your church culture. Candidates may have character and competence, but if you feel they aren't going to mesh with the other staff members, don't hire them. My experience has always been that chemistry matters. If people don't get along, they aren't going to operate at full speed. So, as the saying goes, "The best time to fire someone is before your hire them." (See chapter twenty-three for more on firing.)

Loyalty Rules

I have a speech I give to every person I interview and subsequently hire. It goes something like this: "When it's all said and done here, loyalty rules. You can make mistakes, and we will help you learn from them. However, loyalty is a non-negotiable. Once loyalty is violated, the relationship is over. It may seem harsh, but I need every staff member to know I will be fiercely loyal to him or her, and he or she, in turn, must be loyal to us. Some scoff at this and say it's asking people to be 'yes men,' but I believe it's asking people for unity. Jesus said, 'If a house is divided against itself, that house cannot stand' (Mark 3:25). I have no problem with staff members disagreeing, but when the meeting is over, and we have decided on a direction, then we are loyal to each other and to God's vision for our church."

My best and worst decisions have come in the area of hiring. For that reason, I am purposely slow in hiring. The worst time to hire is when you feel you "have to" get someone in the door. So, purpose in your heart that you will take the time to hire the best person for your church—someone who will enhance an already talented staff.

"You only hire two types of people!" People are usually surprised when I say this because people are so diverse. Some object and tell me that, based on personality types and spiritual gift mixes, there are infinite types of people. While I agree with this, I still come back to my basic premise. As an employer, you only hire two types of people: products and projects. That's it. Both are unique and offer very different perspectives, leadership, and assistance to your organization, but if you are going to hire well, then you need to know what you are getting.

CHAPTER 16
You Only Hire Two Types of People

"You only hire two types of people!" People are usually surprised when I say this because people are so diverse. Some object and tell me that, based on personality types and spiritual gift mixes, there are infinite types of people. While I agree with this, I still come back to my basic premise. As an employer, you only hire two types of people: products and projects. That's it. Both are unique and offer very different perspectives, leadership, and assistance to your organization, but if you are going to hire well, then you need to know what you are getting.

Products

Products are the people who are already highly developed. We could liken "products" to a baseball team that signs a high profile, highly productive free agent. The team knows what they are getting because they have already seen the player produce. In the church world, products are those who are already getting great results in a church environment and when added to your team, they step up to the plate and start hitting the ball out of the park. This person does not need major amounts of time and training invested in them so they can function effectively in their position. They walk into your environment ready to start scoring runs. This person has the gifts, experience, and drive needed to accomplish what you are hiring them to do.

Projects

Projects are the people you see in your organization that have an enormous amount of undeveloped potential. You see the value they could add to your organization with the right time, training, and coaching. These people have a heart for God and come to us from all different lifestyles. Here's the reality—everyone was once a project. The issue is, some have been taken under the wing of an experienced leader and are now products; others are yet to experience that level of training, and you have the opportunity to mold and shape that person's ministry philosophy. From my experience, the greatest players in any church or organization have been projects that a pastor mentored and developed into an amazing product who understand the church's vision and mission. They have a tremendous loyalty towards the one who invested so much to train and develop them that it creates an allegiance to uphold the vision of the church that influenced and blessed them.

So which do you need? That's up to you. What I will tell you is this—projects don't cost as much financially. They can come to us in the form of interns, Bible college graduates, and even the business community. Where they do cost is in the area of time and training. One word of caution—projects can have learning curves in significant areas. Early on, it may feel as though you hired someone to alleviate the load, but since he or she joined your staff, you are working twice as hard. It has happened to me, and I'm sure it will again. Products are "plug and play"; they will make a significant contribution from day one, whereas projects will require attention if you are going to harness all the potential they have for the good of the organization. I believe that in any organization, both are necessary. Just be sure you know which you are getting before you say, "You're hired!"

CHAPTER 17
Potential vs. Proven Performance

I believe one of the many gifts pastors possess is the ability to see the untapped potential in people. In my experience, pastors and church leaders can identify the gifts and talents in people long before they see it in themselves. Yet, here is the warning for those of us who possess this skill—never put someone in a position of leadership and influence without seeing him or her demonstrate proven godly character.

The challenge every church leader faces is one of vast ministry opportunity with a shortage of ministry workers. I have been in full-time church work for a third of my life and have yet to hear a pastor say, "We don't need any more volunteers. We're totally booked." In fact, reality is just the opposite. Usually, there are few serving the needs of many and filling multiple holes.

Many volunteers remind me of the butler in the Adam Sandler movie Mr. Deeds who showed up everywhere there was a need. When asked how he could be so many places at once, he simply replied that he was, "Very, very sneaky." I think most of us would say our volunteers are very, very faithful. So, when there's another hole to fill, and we see someone who possesses tremendous potential, our first inclination is to engage this person and see him or her use his or her gifts.

Yet, this is where I want to caution you. First, let me say that I believe anyone can serve somewhere. In fact, we have been known to allow people to serve in our church who aren't yet following Jesus. Why do we do this? We have found when a person builds a relationship with other Christians, it creates an environment for them to make a decision for Christ. However, a person cannot move beyond an entry-level position before they have to settle the salvation issue.

The purpose of this chapter is to deal with a different group of people. The people we are discussing are Christians, but they still aren't sold out in their relationship with Jesus Christ. In fact, truth be told, there are many areas of their lives where they haven't allowed Jesus to take control. But here's the catch—they are incredibly gifted. Perhaps he is a talented guitar player, and you desperately need a worship leader or key musician. Maybe she is a gifted teacher, and you need someone to fill in for you or lead a small group. Where the rubber meets the road is when you have a hole that needs to be filled, and he or she is the only person in sight to fill the gap. What do you do in these moments? Here is my exhortation to you—go without rather than compromise. I won't tell you this decision is easy, but it's best in the end. Allow them to serve in entry-level positions, but if they aren't committed to waling with Jesus, putting them in positions of leadership are disasters waiting to happen.

One Easter Sunday, early in our history, our band was set to play, and the night before, our drummer called and started flaking out. He started talking negatively about the church, and his true colors were showing through. So, our worship leader made the tough call of telling him that he wasn't playing on Easter. The problem was that he was the only drummer we had in those days.

Our worship leader called me the night before Easter, told me the story, and I commended him for his courage to make the right choice, even though it was obviously going to hurt us on the biggest Sunday of the year. The reason we were able to make this choice so quickly was that there had been times we hadn't made the tough call sooner. We had chosen potential over proven character, and the result was disaster every time. Why is this always disaster? It is because the person who lacks character is given a platform beyond what his or her character can sustain. This lack of character coupled with a leadership position makes him or her a perfect candidate for Satan to use in creating dissension in the church through gossip, backbiting, and negative attitude.

Some of the greatest hurts in my ministry have been over this issue. They have come in moments when I thought I was doing someone a favor by placing him in a position that was beyond his character. While this may be the most difficult thing asked of you as a leader, your best course of action is to give this person time to prove his godly character before being placed in a position of leadership. Paul told Timothy that an elder, "must not be a recent convert, or he may become conceited and fall under the same judgment as the devil" (1 Tim. 3:6, NIV).

The truth is that when we want to do something in our churches and don't see the person who could lead it, there's usually a timing problem. My timing and God's timing aren't aligned. Every time I have run ahead of God when there hasn't been a leader, I have regretted it. The Bible has a word for running ahead of God's timing—Ishmael (Gen. 18). And just like Ishmael, the result in these situations is a mess that takes way too much time to clean up.

CHAPTER 18
Creative Staffing

I've never met a church leader who didn't need more staff or more resources to accomplish what God had called them to do. There always seems to be more opportunity than there is money and more work than there are gifted people to get the job done. I am yet to find a solution to the first problem (short of printing my own currency), but I have found a way to help solve the second problem. I call it creative staffing. We staff positions with five types of people that make it easier on the budget and maximize the gifts of each staff member.

Full-time Staff Members

This is the most common type of staff position. Yet, too many times, churches hire people for only one skill. In his book The Ten Faces of Innovation, Tom Kelley talks about what he calls "T-shaped people." These people have one area of expertise or depth (hence the lower bar of the letter "T") and other areas of expertise, only to a lesser degree (the top bar of the letter "T"). I was speaking with two pastors recently who both hired a worship leader. Both worship leaders were very gifted, yet the first pastor hired a worship leader who could do nothing but music. He didn't possess any other areas of gifting, outside of his musical ability.

The second pastor hired a worship leader who was also gifted as a musician but possessed leadership skills in managing people and casting vision to potential volunteers. It was almost as though he had hired three people instead of one. Needless the say, the first pastor was highly frustrated when his new staff member bought no other skills to the table. So, look for people who have not just one area of expertise, but several gifts they bring to the table when hiring someone full-time.

Part-time Staff Members

In this commonly used hiring strategy, we hire staff for twenty hours a week and give them offices and areas of responsibility. In many cases, if I had the option of hiring one person full time or two people part time, I would opt for two people. The reason is gifting. Two people bring a variety of gifts, experience, and knowledge to the table. Finding part-time staff with a twenty-hour-a-week commitment is a challenge, but they are out there and can really be assets to your team.

Part-time/ Specialist Staff Members

This type of staff member is not utilized enough in churches. In this case, we find people with an expertise in a specialized area, and we hire them part-time to use their skills for the church.

These people usually keep no office hours, but instead work in their off-hours after their "real" jobs are done.

Two areas to consider utilizing this type of hiring are media and graphics. You give the people the projects you need completed, and they go to work on them. Our worship arts pastor supervises them and gives them the input and direction they need, but for the most part, they work on their own. This gives them the freedom they need, and it gives the church the media it needs without having to hire a company every time a video needs to be produced or a graphic needs to be created.

Part-time/ Generalist Staff Members

This type of staff hiring is the one I see used the least. There are areas in your church where you can hire someone for $50–$100 a week and get an incredible return on your investment. We do this with college students and adults whom we trust but want to increase their level of accountability. I have seen churches use this type of staff person as set-up and tear-down team leaders in portable churches, sound engineers, and even key children's ministry positions. These staff members are usually low-cost and high-impact. Like all part-time positions, they serve as a training ground for those who could serve as full-time staff in the future.

Non-paid Staff Members

The non-paid staff member isn't a new designation for a volunteer. This is someone who isn't paid by the church yet adds tremendous value to the organization because of his or her commitment to the church by owning an area of ministry or responsibility that would otherwise have to be filled by a paid staff member. This person doesn't have to be asked to do something; he or she simply takes charge and does it. We have several of these people in our church. They have keys to our office and, at times, arrive before the staff does. Some of these faithful servants are future full-time staff members; others have no desire to leave their careers, yet have a passion for the areas of responsibility entrusted to them.

Staffing has been, and will always be, one of the most important areas for growing churches. I encourage you not to limit yourself to one type of staff hire. Instead, utilize all five types and see your effectiveness grow exponentially.

CHAPTER 19
Tell Your Staff Where They Stand

In any church situation, all staff members believe the ministries they oversee are extremely important to the overall success of the church. I mean, why wouldn't they think so? They spent the best hours of their week investing in an area of ministry that is meeting needs in the lives of people throughout the church and community. But here is where the waters of church world can get a little muddy. What happens when decisions have to be made regarding resources, personnel, or space? What ministry area gets priority? Is this something that happens in an arbitrary manner, or does the staff member with the most "seniority" break the tie?

I believe the best way to fix this potential problem is to address it before it happens. The way we have chosen to address this at Calvary Fellowship is to let our staff and leaders know that while every ministry area matters, not every area is mission critical and, therefore, will not receive the same level of support.

In most churches, children's ministry is vital to families deciding to make your church their home. So, the children's ministry is a top tier program that you want to resource. Therefore, when the singles ministry wants space for an event, and the children's ministry needs another classroom, the decision is a simple one—the children win. This should be common knowledge among your staff. When I was on staff at a large church, I was told that the Bible college I had the privilege of running was sixth on the list of importance. This meant that the church services, worship, children's and youth ministries, the elementary school, and pastoral care ministries were ahead of me. This made sense to me. I recognized, even though I was passionate about training men and women for future ministry, that having church on Sunday took precedence. What I am asking is that every senior leader do this for his or her staff.

When I did this for my staff, no one was really shocked. They weren't thrown for a loop when I told them our youth ministry had higher priority than our café. Yet what it did was show them where they stood in fulfilling the overall mission of the church and what degree of commitment we had for the other ministry environments. What this also did was show my staff on what they were going to be graded. If someone was overseeing three ministry areas: an "A" ministry and two "C" ministries, the bulk of their time should be spent on the "A" ministry because that is the area most critical to the overall success of the church.

If you never lay this out to your team, they will assume either all their areas of oversight are equal, or that the area they enjoy

the most is the one in which they should spend most of their time. The last thing I want my staff to feel is that they worked hard but not in the place that mattered most. So, as the leader, I must tell my staff what the "win" is for them at our church.
If I don't clarify this, the staff will either decide for themselves what the "win" is or become discouraged not knowing where the church is headed.

Let me also say that this will change with time. As your church grows, your staff begins to specialize more, and God entrusts you with a bigger annual budget, you will have the ability to start new ministries. Yet, the key is to keep your eye on what the most important areas are and always resource those most because that is where the greatest results will take place. The payoff is this—your staff will ultimately thank you for being upfront with them and setting clear goals for the church.

CHAPTER 20
Giving People Rest

During the first six months of planting Calvary Fellowship, I took two days off. I don't mean two days off a week. I mean in that six-month period, I took two days off: Christmas Day and New Year's Day. Do you know what happened after those six months? I got so sick that I spent a week in bed! God created us to work six days and rest on the seventh day. God built this rhythm into the makeup of our world. Not only are we to take a sabbath, but also the very land was to be given a sabbath every seven years (Lev. 25:4). Every seventh year, the people of Israel were to take the year off, and after seven cycles of seven years, in the fiftieth year, there was to be a jubilee year where everyone took the year off and simply rejoiced (Lev. 25:12).

The point is, rest is serious business to God. Yet, here is what I have learned in my experience: While God takes rest very seriously; most pastors do not. That's why I see pastors and staff members worn out, wiped out, and burnt out. The tragedy is that all of it could be averted. Rather than belabor the point of all the "rest" infractions I've seen, let me lay out for you what I believe to be proper rest for pastors and church staff members:

Two Days Off a Week

Some might say, "God only took one day off, so that's what I do!" Remember, when a person has a day off from work, most of the time they aren't hanging out at the beach having drinks with umbrellas in them. Most people are cutting their lawns, getting their oil changed, doing some household repair, cleaning the house, going food shopping, or some other activity that doesn't sound much like resting. When you give someone two days off a week, you are ensuring that he or she will have one day actually to rest and not fall victim to the "Honey Do" list. Will there be times when he or she can't have two days off? Of course! But this is the exception rather than the rule.

Generous Vacation Time

Every time I talk to pastors who only give five days of vacation to their staff members, no matter how long they have served..., well, let's just say, it makes me think bad thoughts. Here's my philosophy: A rested staff is a more productive staff. People don't have innovative solutions to problems when they're tired. They might still answer the phone; they just won't have anything of value to say after the word, "Hello." People need at least two weeks of vacation. Please note the words "at least" in the last sentence. Ministry is very rewarding, but anyone who has been in ministry longer than twenty minutes knows how draining it can be. We need time to recharge our batteries and reconnect with our family.

Holiday Trades

I know I'm getting a bit technical here, but at Calvary Fellowship, if July 4 falls on a Monday, and that's someone's day off, he or she can trade that holiday for another day since the national holiday fell on their normal day off. Why do this? Because we don't want to penalize people in ministry for working weekends and having days off during the week. This trade may give the person an extra day to spend with his or her kids, and it shows people that you care about them.

Here's the heart of the matter: the people on our staff are constantly giving of themselves for the kingdom of God. Why not reward their faithfulness by allowing them to rest? There are two huge benefits to this: you get a happier staff member and he or she gets the feeling of knowing the pastor really cares for him or her. In my book, that's called a win-win.

CHAPTER 21
Let Your Wife Be Herself

Have you ever tried to drive your car after someone else has driven it? It's an annoying experience. I can always tell when my wife has been driving my car. The seat is closer to the steering wheel, the A/C vents are shut, and (gasp) the radio station has been changed. The reason the seat is moved is that no two people are exactly alike—even a pastor and his wife. Being a pastor's wife is not an easy task. She carries much of the responsibility of her husband yet none of the authority. She lives with a constant sense that everyone is watching how she treats her family, how she looks, and how she serves in the church. So much has changed in churches over the last twenty years, but in many cases, little has changed for pastors' wives. They're still required to sing, play the piano, run the children's ministry, speak at all the women's ministry events, and of course, do it all with beauty and grace.

In every meeting I have with church planters, they ask me many questions, and I generally let them drive the conversation, but I make sure to talk to them about one area—the role of the pastor's wife. I do this because I believe there are three things every pastor needs to know about his wife. If he fails to acknowledge or understand them, they will hurt his marriage and his ministry.

Your Wife Isn't the Female Version of You

Your wife has a unique set of gifts that aren't a duplicate of yours. Just because you find it easy to communicate to large groups of people, that doesn't mean your wife does also. Yet repeatedly, I see pastors pushing their wives to lead women's ministries and teach groups even when it isn't their natural gifting. If your wife doesn't have an administrative gift, putting her in charge of your children's ministry isn't going to be a good idea long term. Once you realize your wife is different from you, the church will notice this with time. If you allow her to be herself, she will find her place naturally.

Let Her Find Her Place Naturally

My wife oversaw our children's ministry when we first started our church. Later, she started teaching Bible studies for women. However, she didn't feel called to lead a women's ministry. Instead, her gifting was in video production. So, Carey became our first video producer and wrote, shot, and edited nearly every video shown our church in those early years. She would still be producing videos today had she not discovered the joys of motherhood when our daughter came into our lives. My point is that it might take a pastor's wife some time to find her niche. Give her the space to do what she loves and to serve where she feels she can add the most value.

Let her put family first

While I want my wife and the wives of my assistant pastors to be an example of servanthood, I also want them to put family first. Ministry is a wonderful calling, but with it, comes the drain of dealing with the extreme highs and lows of walking with people through their best and worst times. This reality requires home to be a sanctuary and refuge for every minister. I tell the pastor's wives on our staff that the most effective ministry they can have is the unique calling of ministering to their husbands. When I arrive at church on Sunday, people aren't there to meet my needs. God has called me to minister to them. Yet, my wife feels her primary ministry is to care for me as I care for God's people. Few see this role, yet all feel its effects. There are times I just need someone to talk to or encouragement, and my wife has been that person repeatedly. The greatest gift she has given me is a home that is a sanctuary where I can rest, be refreshed, be loved, and then lead where God is calling our church to go next. So let your wife blossom where she's planted, and you will find that the person you're married to is happier, contributing more, and supporting to an even greater degree than you thought possible.

CHAPTER 22
The Leader who Gets to Carry a Guitar

Let me start out by saying that I am a musician. I've been playing in bands since I was sixteen years old. One of my bands had a record deal on Tooth and Nail records where we released two successful albums. When I became a Christian, I believed God would lead me to be a worship leader. It wasn't until I discovered I had a teaching gift that I saw God moving me in another direction. I say all of this because what I am about to say might be slightly offensive to some, unspiritual to others, and irrelevant to those who have no contact with worship leaders. If you're in the last group, feel free to skip this chapter. (I hear chapter twenty-three is riveting.)

The conflict between senior pastors and worship pastors is well documented for all generations to see. The senior pastor wants to change something at the last minute, and the worship pastor gets upset because the senior pastor is being unreasonable. After this exchange, the senior pastor wonders what the worship pastor actually does forty to forty-five hours a week. Yet, even the mention of accounting for his time causes the worship pastor to go over the edge.

Brace for Impact

Here's what many churches have: a worship pastor who thinks he's a rock star. This is the reason he won't do anything unrelated to his area of oversight. It's also why he cops an attitude when you ask him to cut a song or change something in the worship set. Here's the real kicker: Do you know who is to blame for this? The senior pastor. "Rock star" worship leaders have usually been enabled by pastors who don't want to rock the boat because they love the music on Sunday. The problem occurs because senior pastors don't get worship leaders more involved in the ministry of the church. Thus, they become islands unto themselves, playing guitar in their dimly lit office, dreaming of the day they write a hit song that every church in America will be singing.

All sarcasm aside, the senior pastor has to take responsibility for cultivating the relationship between pastor and worship leader. He must take several steps to ensure this relationship is the healthiest relationship on the staff.

A Passion for Evangelism

The worship pastor needs to have the same intensity for evangelism that the senior pastor has. If not, worship leaders can fall into the trap of, "Let's forget about time constraints and attention spans. Let's just worship the Lord." When the worship leader turns inward, the rest of the church begins to do the same. A worship leader with a passion for evangelism scans the crowd on Sunday and looks to see how guests are connecting with the songs. Song choice is a great indicator of where a worship pastor's heart is. Is he choosing songs that he believes the whole church will connect with or a song he just likes to play?

Mark Rodriguez, worship pastor at Calvary Fellowship is the best at this skill. Many times, I will hear a song and recommend it to him. At times, he will listen to it and point out words in the song that aren't part of normal English vernacular. He is so passionate about reaching people and engaging them in worship that he'd rather sacrifice a song he likes for the sake of finding another song everyone will understand. He is famous for saying, "I love the song, but it won't work for us."

100 Percent Buy-in to the Church

Too many worship leaders see themselves as "free agents" just waiting for the next gig. The best worship pastors are those who love their church. They believe in the vision of the church. Our worship pastor is as committed to the vision of our church as I am. This isn't just the church where he works; this is the church where he is contributing his part to see all of Miami reached with the Gospel. If the worship pastor isn't totally committed, he should find a place where he is 100 percent committed.

They Are Great Leaders as Well as Great Worship Leaders

A big mistake senior pastors make is not giving worship leaders more responsibility. Worship leaders need to be developed into leaders in non-music areas of the church as well. I have long held the belief that being a worship leader is not a full-time job. It's part of a full-time job, but you can't tell me that choosing, rehearsing, and performing songs takes forty-five hours a week. There comes a point where as a church grows, being a worship pastor becomes a full-time job, but not at a church of one hundred. I believe a church with attendance under two thousand people can grow with a worship pastor who has responsibilities outside of the music department. This is not only good stewardship; it also helps the worship leader develop into a better leader.

Involved in the Creative Process

One of the gifts worship pastors bring to the table is creativity. Senior pastors should lean on worship leaders for help and input in this area. Get your worship leader involved in the creative process. Let them know where the next series of messages is going early enough, so they can plan and bring music that complements each message. This has become popular in recent days, but in many circles, the worship leader's and the senior pastor's worlds rarely meet. And if per chance, the songs line up with the topic of the message, then we know "it was the Lord." When the worship leader and senior pastor meet to plan services, they work together to see the service as one cohesive unit, not two separate pieces duct taped together.

Loyal to a Fault

There should be no bad blood, gossip, or backbiting between the senior pastor and worship pastor. Pastors should be loyal to their worship leaders and never speak ill of them. Worship leaders should respect their pastor and express their loyalty by believing the best in their pastor and standing by their pastor. When loyalty and trust are broken, it is extremely difficult for this relationship to work. Worship leaders need to understand the level of trust that has been given to them. They have been entrusted with 50 percent of the Sunday service. The response to that kind of trust should be loyalty. If you can't be loyal to your pastor, then you need to resign immediately.

I know I've come on stronger in this chapter more than in others. Here's the reason why: Many people in your church believe the church is the pastor and the worship leader. They don't know any of the other staff members and leaders. At our church, people know Bob and Mark. This is what makes the position of worship leader so unique. It is a highly visible role where you are given a great deal of spiritual authority. We must steward that authority with wisdom and grace, never using it to cut down the person who gave us the position in the first place. The bottom line is this: Show me a strong church, and I will show you a strong relationship between the pastor and worship leader. If you want a strong, healthy church, strengthen the relationship between the senior pastor and the worship pastor.

CHAPTER 23
The One Thing You Don't Want to do

One of the biggest challenges of leadership is dealing with underperforming staff. Few church leadership issues will give you more indigestion, headaches, and sleepless nights than staffing problems. I know of churches that have specific ministries that serve as an "island of the misfit toys" for staff that aren't pulling their weight. These leaders won't release these underperforming staff members, which in the end hurts their organizations and the individuals in question. How to deal with people who aren't a good fit for your organization in a way that's right for the church and treats the individual with respect is an important balance. In my years as a leader, I have observed four key strategies to handling staff problems.

Deal with Problems When They Happen

One of the mistakes that are common with many leaders is a tendency not to deal with problems as they happen. If we're a little more formal in our structure, there will be a problem, and our reaction will be, "It's May, but I'm going to write this down because I'm going to deal with this issue during their December review." I believe you can't wait to handle infractions. The more serious the issue, the quicker it needs to be dealt with. If a staff member isn't keeping up with the rest of the staff in relation to job performance, this must be confronted immediately. If you hesitate, you are sending a message to the rest of the staff that this kind of behavior is acceptable. In addition, you are sending an equally misleading message to the staff member in question that their ineffectiveness is tolerated and encouraged.

The same is true with behavioral problems. A leader who will not deal with a staff member who disrespects the senior leadership of the church, disagrees with the church's primary mission, or simply has a bad attitude is inviting discord onto his team. When leaders handle such problems quickly, decisively, and effectively, they are showing the rest of the team how serious these infractions are and that there is zero tolerance for such behavior.

Can They Be Reassigned?

Sometimes, an underperforming staff member is simply in the wrong position. Many times, this can be resolved by moving the person into a different position. When someone is the right person but in the wrong position, he will usually have to stay late to keep up with the rest of the team. This does not mean he isn't giving his best. Rather, he will be working hard but will have difficulty keeping up. A person who isn't giving 100 percent doesn't need to reassigned; they need to be released. A lack of gifting is not an excuse for laziness. Laziness is a cancer for any staff. When a person doesn't put forth his or her best effort, it sends a message to everyone on the team. The message is, "It's OK if you don't put forth your best effort here. There aren't any repercussions for not doing your best." I know you don't want to send that message to anyone, much less your team. If the person in question is in the wrong position, transfer them. If the problem is lack of performance, the person needs to be fired.

"You're Fired"

I've only had to say these words a couple of times, and it never gets easy. In fact, even when the person had been disrespectful to me and had grossly underperformed, it was still difficult to say the words. Here's what I encourage you to do: Bring the person into your office, and tell them they have been terminated. Don't say it in anger. Instead, communicate in a very calm voice. You should speak confidently but without gloating or spite. This person is about to enter one of the most stressful times in his or her life. For that reason alone, we should treat him or her with respect.

A Parting Gift

Severance can be given, but it isn't mandatory. A best practice in many business circles is to give a week's severance pay for every year served. However, these are guidelines, not hard and fast rules. If the person being released has been respectful and loyal to the organization, then severance may be the fair course to pursue. However, if the person has been a destructive force on your team, you should not feel any obligation to give any type of severance.

The Best Time to Fire

The old adage is true: the best time to fire someone is before you hire him or her. How can you tell if someone isn't going to work out before hiring them? Look at their job history. Are there gaps of time missing? This may be a sign there is a place of employment they want to hide. When calling previous employers, listen to not only what people are saying, but also what they aren't saying. If they aren't saying, "_____ was a very hard worker. _____ didn't leave until the job was completed. _____ worked well with his fellow team members. I'd love to have _____ back." You may have a future problem employee on your hands.

Firing a person is serious business because it is going to affect that person's life drastically. Will it give you sleepless nights, headaches, and indigestion as you agonize before making the decision? Let's just say you should stop at a drugstore before heading home from the office.

CHAPTER 24
Brick Layers and Bible Teachers

The only people who say leading a church is easy are those who have never done it. Unlike most organizations that can influence people through a paycheck or some other financial incentive, churches must influence most through a compelling vision. This is especially seen when it comes to mobilizing people for ministry. It is neither possible nor biblical for a church to employ every person who serves in some capacity. Yet, it is vital for every person to have a role that matters in the fulfilling of the Great Commission.

Ask the Question, "How Many?"

Churches tend to run on a scarcity mentality. They only ask, "How few do we need to get the job done?" when moving into a new area of ministry. Instead, why not ask, "How many can get plugged in?" and see the new area as an opportunity for the unengaged to get involved. This change in thinking alone has the power to transform how you view the opportunities you can create in your ministry.

Everyone Should Have a Role

I am a firm believer in the priesthood of all believers. That is, I believe every Christian has access to God and that every Christian has the privilege of serving God. Prior to Jesus' ministry and the establishment of the Church, priests were the only ones who served God "officially" in the Temple in Jerusalem. They worked on a rotation, so every priest could serve, but when it was all said and done, thousands were standing on the sidelines while a select few were experiencing the blessing of serving. The New Testament writers saw every believer in Jesus as a priest (1 Peter 2:5-9) and, thus, every believer having the honor of serving God. That is why I encourage people to serve God in the church. When people are serving God, they are fulfilling roles for which they were created.

Ask!

The reason many people in your church haven't started serving is that they haven't been asked. The tricky part is that not every "ask" is the same. Some people respond based on an announcement that is made from the stage. Others respond to a post on your Web site or bulletin. Still others respond only when they are personally invited and encouraged to use their gifts in a particular area of ministry. The moral of the story is that we need to ask. Ask in different ways. Ask at different times. Have different people ask. The result will be greater congregational involvement and thus, greater opportunity for your church to reach its full redemptive potential.

The Law of Building a Cathedral

The story is told of two men working on a building. One is asked what he is doing. He responds, "I'm laying bricks." The second is asked the same question, and he responds, "I'm building a cathedral for God." While both men were doing the same task, they saw their activity from very different perspectives. As leaders, we must tie every activity in our churches back to the big vision of honoring God and reaching people. If not, people are just "laying bricks."

I am regularly sharing with our greeters, parking lot team, and ushers that they are preaching the message every bit as much as I am. I believe if a person isn't greeted warmly and shown that we care they arrived, it makes my job much harder when I teach the Scriptures. A bad experience will close them off to the Gospel (or at least hearing it at our church). Yet, when a person has a great experience, they are more open because they have seen the Gospel in the lives of our volunteers. When a person sees himself or herself as "just a greeter," "just an usher," or "just a set-up person," they are missing out on the joy of serving. We must help people see that what they do, no matter how small, is all part of God's plan to reach our city in which each of us is playing a role.

My first ministry experience was setting up chairs and making coffee on Sunday mornings for a new believers class. I arrived at church at 6:30 AM to start brewing the coffee. Then I would put the chairs in rows and pray over one, asking God to bless the person that would sit there. Later, I graduated to teaching that new believers class. Then lastly, I was ordained as a pastor in that same church. I remember the first night I preached in that church. Thirty-five hundred people attended that night, and over fifty people gave their lives to Jesus Christ as I preached the Gospel. Here's what I know to be true: God was using me when I was making coffee and when I was teaching the Scriptures. The only difference was the visibility and influence of my ministry. All of us are "laying bricks" in our own way as we build God's cathedral together.

CHAPTER 25
Create a Farm System

Two decisions, like no others, have affected my life as a follower of Jesus. The first was when I decided to honor God with my finances. I heard a pastor speak boldly from God's Word in regards to tithing, and I decided to take God at His Word and try it. Years have past, and all I can say is that God has been so faithful to me. The second decision was the choice to roll up my sleeves to get involved in the church that I called home. I know this might not be the end all in regards to service as we look at a world that is desperately in need of practical ministry, but I do believe that serving in a simple capacity at church on a Sunday can begin to get people to live beyond themselves.

As pastors, we need to facilitate this by casting a strong vision of what it means to follow Jesus. We hear so much these days about the need to cast vision for a building program, a new ministry venture, or a strategic change that we need to make. Yet I hear too little talk of what the world could look like if God's people started truly following Jesus. Let me say at the onset that this is going to take guts. People, especially in America, don't want to hear about a faith that involves taking up your cross and following Jesus. Yet, this is the message we preach. If we choose simply to let people sit in rows every seven days and call that the Christian faith, then we have done both Jesus and His church a great disservice.

Having said that, let me say that I believe begging for volunteer help is a sign of a much deeper problem. If a church cannot get anyone to serve in its youth ministry, then there are bigger problems than a teenager with no one to toss a football. There is a discipleship problem here that must be addressed or people will "help out," but not really serve. If you have led people for any length of time, then you know there's a difference between "helping out" and serving Jesus. The main difference is in the area of focus. Those who help out look to the church or the ministry leader as the one they are assisting. They like you, so they show up and give you a hand as you serve. Those that serve, on the other hand, look to Jesus as the One they serve. If the ministry leader changes, or they are asked to do something else, their focus remains the same.

Our role as pastors is to make disciples, and that involves servanthood. People who serve only in the area they feel "called to" might be very talented, but they lack the heart of the One who got on His knees to wash the feet of His disciples. I look for this quality in potential staff members. I look for people who don't say, "Well, that's not my job!" I have never met people who truly felt that their calling was to take out garbage and sweep floors.

Yet, I know countless servants who do, not out of a sense of gifting for the "custodial arts" (to quote John Bender from The Breakfast Club), but out of a calling to do whatever they can for the God who has done so much for them. The Jews looked on this type of person and said, "These who have turned the world upside down have come here too. Jason has harbored them, and these are all acting contrary to the decrees of Caesar, saying there is another king—Jesus" (Acts 17:6–7, NKJV).

At the same time, it is important for us to be strategic and give people entry points that help individuals take the first steps in their path of discipleship. These entry points can be as simple as greeting those that come to church and handing them a bulletin, helping with the set-up and tear-down of our portable church, or assisting a children's ministry teacher in a classroom. I find many churches tend to do this, but few think through what is strategically necessary to see people stretched beyond that. As an avid baseball fan, I tend to think of everything in terms of how a big league team is structured. We can usually identify those that are at the big league level (pastors, staff, elders, deacons) and those who serve at what we call "Single A" (entry level ministry positions). But the challenge for every church is to lead those at "Single A" to "Double A," those in "Double A" to "Triple A," and those in "Triple A" to the majors. You have to wrestle through the same Scriptures we did to determine when, why, and how people move from one level of responsibility to the next. The Apostle John recognized that not everyone in the church was at the same level of maturity and responsibility.

I write to you, little children, because your sins are forgiven you for His name's sake. I write to you, fathers, because you have known Him who is from the beginning. I write to you, young men, because you have overcome the wicked one. I write to you, little children, because you have known the Father. I have written to you, fathers, because you have known Him who is from the beginning. I have written to you, young men, because you are strong, and the word of God abides in you, and you have overcome the wicked one. (1 John 2:12–14, NKJV)

So how do you move people from Single A to the major leagues? It takes time, gifting, and proven character to discern when it's time to move someone up a level.

Tick Tock

Every personnel mistake I have ever made with volunteers has been because I neglected one of these areas. I wish people could be evaluated like baseball players. You see them, and a graphic appears that says they're batting .305 with twenty-five home runs and eighty-five RBI's. Unfortunately, it doesn't work that way. Yet, think of it this way: time always reveals a person's true colors. Many people talk a good game, but time will tell you who they are. Time will also show you if this person is faithful or not.

A Gift for You

In the same way, gifting will tell you if people have the God-given gifts to get the job done. They might be the most faithful persons in the world, but if they don't have the gifts to get the job done, they aren't going to excel.

You're a Character

Lastly, proven character will show you how serious they are about their faith. Watch how they love their wives, treat their kids, and speak to others. Then, you'll see if these people are ready to go to the next level. I encourage you to make it easy for people to get involved and serve but gradually turn up the heat and increase the intensity of their service and the level of commitment.

Churches who take service seriously have more mature people than those who take a more casual approach. My desire is to have a church where those who serve always have a next step in their service— where they can grow to become the people God wants them to be. Take service seriously, and committed people will be the least of your problems.

CHAPTER 26
Ask!

If you are a leader, then you are in the business of asking. You are asking people to make a decision to follow Jesus. You are asking people to grow to greater levels of commitment. You are asking people to sacrifice for the mission of the church. Let's be honest: If you're in ministry, you are a professional "asker." Too many leaders wind up with "Moses syndrome." This is what happened in Exodus 18 when Moses was doing everything himself and his father-in-law had to tell him to ask people to help so the load was manageable. Church leaders are much better at doing than they are at asking. Yet, I have learned that if we overcome the personal roadblocks we put up to asking, we create an opportunity for more people to be involved in the work God is doing in our churches.

The Fear of "No"

I wasn't a great student in school. In fact, I like to say that being a senior was the best two years of my life. When I was finishing the eighth grade and considering high school options, I wanted to go to Boston College High School. My goal was eventually to go on to Boston College where I'd be drafted by the Boston Red Sox and play professional baseball. But here's what stopped me: I couldn't fill out the application to BC High School. Think about it: all the millions of dollars I missed, simply because I didn't fill out an application (lack of talent was another problem, but I digress). I was so afraid they would say no, I never filled out the paperwork.

Here's the reality: Let's say I applied to BC High School, and they said no. Was I accepted to BC High School before I applied? No. Was I accepted after I applied? No. Then, nothing changed by my asking. Many leaders fail to ask people to step up their commitment, to give of themselves, or put their plans on hold for the sake of the kingdom of God because they're afraid of being told no. Your situation is no different before the "no" than it is after the "no." If that's the case, then ask because you may get a yes that changes things drastically.

Speak Their Language

One of the quickest ways to get a "yes" from people is to speak their language. What I mean by this is to frame what you're asking someone to do in a way that speaks to one of his or her core values. For example, as church leaders, we need a steady flow of servants who are willing to take their time and talents and give them to the local church. Yet, when pastors ask their congregations to serve, they get minimal response. Why is this? I believe it is because we haven't touched on people's core values.

What are people's core values? For a Christian, it could be the desire to grow spiritually. So, you might need to teach a message on how emptying yourself through service is how God can fill you with more of Him. You may need to teach a message on how we are the body of Christ, and God has given us gifts so that we can accomplish this great goal of reaching the entire world. Whatever you decide, make sure the request you're making speaks the language of your hearer and your chances of getting a yes goes way up.

Is There a Small Step to Take?

One of the things I like to do is give people small steps to take in saying yes. If we're asking people to serve, I will ask people to commit to serving one hour a month. One hour a month doesn't seem like much, but it gets you into the world of "yes." Once people have begun serving, I am confident they will love it, grow in their faith through their service, and turn that one hour into several hours over the course of time. This can take several forms: it could be asking people to read one chapter of the Bible a day. It could be a charge to pray for five minutes a day. Whatever you're asking, if you can find a way for people to say yes in a small way, it makes the step less scary and more achievable.

Believe in What You're Asking

There is no substitute for believing in what you're asking people to do. If you're asking people to give financially to a building project, and you haven't committed anything, there will be no power in your request. People are looking to follow someone whose life is consistent with his talk. When King David was preparing all of the supplies for the building of the temple, he said, "'Moreover, because I have set my affection on the house of my God, I have given to the house of my God, over and above all that I have prepared for the holy house, my own special treasure of gold and silver...Who then is willing to consecrate himself this day to the LORD?' Then the leaders of the fathers' houses, leaders of the tribes of Israel, the captains of thousands and of hundreds, with the officers over the king's work, offered willingly" (1 Chron. 29:3, 5–6). What gave David the authority to make this giant request was his own commitment. If you aren't committed personally, you won't find very many yeses when you ask.

So, don't be shy. Your church needs you to be bold in asking people to do whatever is necessary for the vision God has placed in your heart. You can't do it alone. You're going to need help. So, ask, and ask, and ask, and ask. Then, when you're done asking, ask some more.

CHAPTER 27
Say "Thank You"

"The first role of a leader is to define reality. The last is to say thank you."

—Max Dupree

It is imperative that every leader becomes fluent in the language of thanks. Unfortunately, there seems to be this idea in the church that if we say thank you to those who are serving and giving of themselves each week that somehow they are losing their heavenly reward. Personally, I believe that's a copout from leaders who are either lazy or simply unwilling to express appreciation for the work others are doing in the church. People don't serve because of the thanks we give them. However, many will continue serving because they feel valued by others. The saying is true: "What gets rewarded gets repeated." So, how can we as leaders say thank you to those who serve so faithfully in our churches? We're going to consider five ways.

Using the Words

I have a two-year-old daughter who is learning basic communication. She knows how to say what she wants but is now learning how to show gratitude when her needs are met. In the same way, leaders need to become fluent in saying "thank you." The reason we need to say thank you is not that these amazing people are serving us in some way. On the contrary, they are serving the Lord. Yet as a pastor and a leader, it matters when we say thank you to those who are giving of themselves each week in the churches and organizations we oversee. Here's my encouragement: Be specific. Don't just say, "Thanks for everything." That's too vague. Specificity gives weight to our gratitude. Instead, say something along the lines of, "Thank you for getting to church at 5 AM on Sunday to unload the trucks." Comments such as these show that we notice what those in our care are doing and that it matters to us.

Writing the Words

I have a practice of writing thank-you cards each week to volunteers who go beyond the call of duty. As Christians, we are all called to serve. Yet, some take their service to an even higher level. I want to express appreciation to those who sacrifice for the cause of the kingdom and the local church. I hear more feedback from the handwritten cards I write than any other single thing I do to express gratitude. I believe it is because people know that writing a card and expressing thoughts on paper takes time. In addition, handwritten cards are out of the ordinary these days. Most people are sending text messages or firing off e-mails, so getting a card that's handwritten stands out.

Showing the Words

One of the things we do at Calvary Fellowship is buying books for those who serve. If I read a book that I believe will benefit those in our church, I will buy multiple copies and mail them to our servants. We normally don't buy hundreds of copies and give them to every volunteer, but within our church are different volunteer teams. We will buy books or give teaching CD's to the group or groups in our church that we are seeking to bless. Once again, people don't serve in order to get a $20 book. The book is simply a token of appreciation to those who regularly give of themselves.

Sharing the Words Publicly

Another way to say thank you is to recognize people publicly. This is where some might protest and recite the words of Jesus: "Be careful not to do your 'acts of righteousness' before men, to be seen by them. If you do, you will have no reward from your Father in heaven" (Matt. 6:1). The context of this verse is motivation, not thanks. I agree that when a person does anything for being recognized by others, their reward remains here on Earth.

I do not agree with the philosophy that saying anything kind to someone causes a person to "lose his or her reward." I regularly tell our church to thank the children's ministry team who has been teaching their kids while the adults have been enjoying an adult environment where God's Word is taught. We highlight our set-up and tear-down crew who arrive early and stay late every week to make our church services be all they can be in a portable setting. The point is, when you say thank you to your servants publicly, it raises the value of servanthood in the entire church.

Celebrate the Words

Every year, our church hosts a party for every person who serves in our church. It is our way of saying the biggest "thank you" possible for a year of faithful service. On this night, the staff serves the volunteers. We have the event catered by the best barbeque place in the city of Miami; we play hilarious games, give out prizes, and most of all, we provide a time for our team to be appreciated for all they do. I am then able to stand up, share my heart, and remind each of us why we do what we do. These can be the strategic moments for sharing vision with those who have the highest level of buy-in and commitment in the church.

People want to know they are appreciated for all they do. They want to know that what they're doing is making a difference. Saying "thank you" is a simple way to accomplish that big task.

PART 3
Ministry Strategies

CHAPTER 28
Gauges on the Dashboard

We know what numbers such as 98.6 or 120/80 mean—they're gauges of our physical health. Likewise, we look at gauges on the dashboard to see if our car is "healthy"; if something lights up or goes into a red zone, we know there's a problem.

In the same way, churches have metrics—numbers that speak to the health of the body of Christ or to our need for help. The Bible says, "Know well the condition of your flocks, and give attention to your herds" (Prov. 27:23). What are the metrics that can give us a strong indication of the health of a local church body?

I look to the following eight vital signs that speak the language of health or help. One could argue that there are plenty of other valid metrics for a church; I would agree. But just as your car's dashboard gives you the most critical information about the "health" of the engine, these eight metrics will be some of the most important indicators of your church's health, helping you see where attention and energy need to be applied:

Five first-time guests for every one hundred attendees. Plain and simple, churches grow because of first-time guests. So, to measure at what rate your church can grow, see how many first-time guests you're having each weekend. As a rule of thumb, a good goal is five first-time guests for every hundred people in attendance. This will tell you what the evangelistic temperature is at your church. (Note: Just to stay even, due to natural attrition, you normally need at least three first-time guests for every hundred attendees.)

One baptized for every three decisions. Not every person who makes a decision for Jesus by walking forward, checking a response-card box, or raising a hand in a service will go on to take the step of baptism. Many factors can keep them from taking that step, but a healthy-sized group of people should understand the significance of baptism and go into the water to declare their faith publicly.

When a pastor is regularly teaching on baptism, providing resources to help people overcomes mental barriers to it, and giving opportunities to take that step of faith, people will be baptized. How many? I believe a good metric is one out of three who make a recorded salvation decision.

Over the years in our church when I've been lacking in teaching on baptism, the number of baptisms has declined considerably. So, I keep watch on this number to help me make sure I'm regularly communicating this command of Jesus.

This week's attendance compared to this week last year. One of the big mistakes I made early on was to gauge how our church was doing on a week-to-week basis. Was attendance better this week than the week before? This kind of measuring can become a roller coaster that drives a pastor crazy. If our week-to-week numbers are up, we're feeling good. If they're down, we're calling ourselves losers all the way home from church. Countless factors can bring weekly changes in these numbers—everything from holidays and school vacations to a strange virus sent by aliens that affects alarm clocks (maybe the last one happened only in my city).

I believe we get a better picture of what's happening in our church by comparing this week's numbers with the same week last year. This will give you the metrics you need to measure health.

For example, comparing the attendance from this Labor Day weekend to Labor Day last year will tell you more about the health of your church than comparing each weekend in September with each other. And since Easter moves around so much on the calendar, always compare this Easter with last Easter rather than with that particular Sunday from last year.

Current giving compared to the same period last year. Likewise, don't measure giving week-to-week, since there are many reasons why giving fluctuates on a weekly basis. And when it comes to seeing trends, look at the bigger picture. Compare this quarter with this quarter last year, or compare all of this year with all of last year (or previous years). This will give you a much better picture of the condition of your church.

Fifty percent involved in ministry. For believers to grow to maturity, each one must experience both input and outflow. Many Christians are very good at receiving, but churches must emphasize the vital importance—for spiritual development and maturity—of learning to serve and give out.

I believe that when a church has 50 percent of the congregation mobilized for ministry, it's a sign of health. What does this ministry involvement include? We define it as "serving someone else in the local church for at least one hour a week." This could be serving at one of our weekend services, hosting or leading a small group, or being involved in some aspect of the church's outreach or evangelism.

Forty percent committed to membership. A church that has 100 percent of its people committed to membership is not a healthy church. That may sound like heresy, but follow my thought: Churches should always have a healthy-sized group of new believers in the crowd. Each week, there should also be people there who aren't even Christians yet and who are considering the claims of Christ. I believe that if a church has less than 40 percent of its attendees going through its membership class, it's a light on the dashboard indicating that something's awry.

This problem could be solved by something as simple as making announcements about the membership class that are more effective or preaching on membership more regularly. Or the solution could be more involved, such as giving the membership class a better format and more dynamic appeal.

100 percent involved in small groups. You probably think the average church in America has more like 20 percent of its people in small groups—so how can 100 percent be a realistic metric? My answer is twofold.

First, the average church is America has an excessive number of events and programs going on, which prevents any reasonable expectation of higher involvement in small groups.

Second, "average" is never the goal (it's so... well, average). Exceptional should be the goal. When a church focuses on small groups and makes this their primary disciple-making tool as well as their engine for reproducing leaders, the percentage of involvement will rise.

50—30—10—10. No, this isn't a code for cheaper long distance rates. It's actually a guideline for budgeting. Since day one at Calvary Fellowship, we've sought to attain these four percentages for our financial resources:

50 percent for staffing.

30 percent for operations and ministry.

10 percent tithe.

10 percent savings.

We haven't always operated exactly at these levels. At times, we've been higher on staffing (which is typical for new church plants), or we've not saved a full 10 percent. But the 50-30-10-10 split has served as our overall operating framework.

CHAPTER 29
Lessons in Outreach

Calvary Fellowship started as a home Bible study with five people. The most daunting task we had early on was figuring out how to let people know we existed. I made the mistake early on of putting all our hopes in one method rather than using different means to communicate who we were as a church and, of course, the message of the Gospel. I see churches make this mistake all the time. They either put eggs in the Easter basket (pun intended) thinking this Super Bowl of Sunday services will attract enough new people to keep the church growing throughout the year. Alternatively, they are "Old School" in their thinking, believing personal evangelism is all that matters and all we need. The key is to do what your friends did in high school when they came to your house to pick you up. They beeped the horn. We beep the horn of the church by using every means available to communicate to our community that we exist so we can introduce them to God who is willing forgive their sins and meet all of their needs.

Here are four ways every church needs to B.E.E.P. the horn to make its presence known:

B — Big Days

These are the natural high days of the church calendar. Some days, such as Easter and Mother's Day, are built into the calendar. Other big days can be manufactured to build momentum and see new people come to the church for the very first time.

E — Evangelism

Nothing can substitute individuals sharing their faith with family, friends, coworkers, and classmates. However, for people to share the Gospel, they must be equipped to do so and given the tools to share the message that has changed their lives.

E — Excellent Weekend Services

To the average person, your church is reduced to one hour on Sunday. The sooner we start taking Sunday more seriously, the better off our church and our community at large will be.

P — Promotion

Personal evangelism is how we reach out to those who are connected to someone in our church; but how do we reach out to those who have no connection to our church whatsoever? The answer is promotion.

Now that you have the outline, I will spend the next four chapters detailing ways your church can utilize each of these ways to let your community know you exist, so you can communicate the message you are called to share.

CHAPTER 30
The Big Ideas on Big Days

We are all influenced by the calendar. We all eat turkey on Thanksgiving, candy on Halloween, and Hershey's kisses on Valentine's Day. The calendar affects all of us; so, instead of fighting the calendar, why not cooperate with it? I believe the calendar can be our greatest ally as we plan our preaching for each year. Then again, what's the alternative? If you fight the calendar, I promise you will lose every time.

I have a friend who pastors a great church (and will remain nameless in the spirit of Joe Friday), and he decided he was going to be the one who fought the calendar and won. He was preaching through the Gospel of Matthew, and although Mother's Day was around the corner, he thought, "I'm just going to teach the next chapter no matter what day it is." So Mother's Day came, and what did he teach to honor all the moms in his church? Matthew 25—the judgment of the nations! After the message, he called me and essentially said, "I fought the calendar, and the calendar won." Since that day, his strategy has completely changed. He teaches on the freedom we have in Christ every July 4, giving thanks every Thanksgiving weekend, and resting in the Lord on Labor Day. The moral of the story is when we teach on what people are already thinking about, we create a connection and are instantly relevant to the listening audience.

So, how do I cooperate with the calendar and use it to my advantage? Here are six dates that will help you in planning your preaching throughout the year:

January. This is a great month to talk about vision, evangelism, finances, getting a fresh start or making changes.

February. I believe this is the best month to teach on relationships. People are naturally thinking about relationships due to Valentine's Day. This can take shape as a marriage series, a study on the Song of Solomon, or a series for single adults.

Easter. Too many pastors only teach on the resurrection on Easter. While this may sound sacrilegious, think about this for a moment. Easter is the one day where you have more guests than any other time of the year. There are people who come to church once a year and hear the same message every time they show up. It's no wonder why they wait another year to return. They think it's the only message we have. I believe we should not only teach on the resurrection, but also teach on the resurrection power that's available to all believers (Rom. 8:11). That is why I encourage you to teach a series of messages geared towards living the Christian life with an emphasis on evangelism on Easter Sunday.

Mother's Day. This may be the most contrarian thing I say in this chapter, but I rarely talk to moms on Mother's Day. Think about it, the moms in your church say one thing to their family on Mother's Day: "All I want for Mother's Day is to go to church with my whole family." If this day is the one time we reach guys who never go to church, I want to teach a message that will connect with them. Therefore, I usually kick off a series on Mother's Day, and I focus on a book of the Bible or topic that will be of particular interest to them. We've launched series on God's will, hearing God's voice, the book of Daniel and the names of God on Mother's Day. My goal is to pique the curiosity of guests in the audience and see them return the next week.

Father's Day. While I rarely teach a traditional Father's Day message, I normally kick off a series on Father's Day. This series or book study is usually more discipleship oriented. An example of this might be a character study on John the Baptist, a series through the Gospel of Mark, or messages on spiritual disciplines.

Fall. People are focused on one thing in the fall—back to school. I graduated a long time ago, and my wife still has to stop me from buying pencils and a backpack every September. The reason is that all of our minds are focused on hitting the books, growing, and learning. So, we cooperate with this by teaching a longer series in the fall with an emphasis on personal and spiritual growth. We have taught through the books of Colossians and Ecclesiastes and done topical series focusing on different areas of spiritual growth in recent history.

You have the freedom to teach on the Levitical dietary laws on Valentine's weekend, or you can use the calendar to your advantage and create a memorable experience that resonates with what people are already thinking about and see the people in your church go farther in their discipleship and outreach than ever before.

CHAPTER 31
A New Way to Look at Your Community

I do not consider myself an evangelist. I am a teacher and a trainer. In fact, every spiritual gifts test I have taken ranks my top three spiritual gifts as teaching, leadership, and administration. Somewhere down the line (I think just before martyrdom and mercy) is where you will find my gift of evangelism. Having said all that, I still believe I have a responsibility to make sure evangelism is happening at Calvary Fellowship. Paul told Timothy, "But you be watchful in all things, endure afflictions, do the work of an evangelist, fulfill your ministry" (2 Tim. 4:5, NKJV). So, while my evangelism gift isn't registering on the Richter scale, I still need to make sure my church is aligned with God's plan in fulfilling the Great Commission.

I need to tell you my story so I can make my point. Calvary Fellowship began in September of 2000 (a great time of year to plant a church by the way) and over the next eighteen months, we did not see one person come to faith in Jesus Christ. We baptized a few people who had never made that decision, but as far as first-time decisions, we looked like the final score at a Kansas City Royals game—0. I was deeply grieved when I was confronted with these facts. I made a decision that I would do whatever it takes for Calvary Fellowship to be a place where people were coming to know Christ every Sunday. This led me to looking at evangelism from a new perspective. I used to see evangelism only in the one-on-one, personal evangelism sense. I still believe this is a vital aspect of evangelism, but other approaches complement the one-on-one approach.

I began looking at my role as a pastor and how I shared the Gospel each week. I began giving a Gospel presentation most Sundays, so our members knew that if they brought their friend to church, they would hear a clear presentation of the Gospel and have an opportunity to respond. I have found that this gives our members confidence in inviting their friends to church, and it creates a less confrontational opportunity for people to take a faith conversation to the next level even if someone isn't ready to give his or her life to Jesus Christ yet. This decision alone radically changed what happened in our church. But there was another decision that helped us as well.

We also began looking at our community in two groups. We saw our community as either 1) knowing someone who attends Calvary Fellowship or 2) not knowing someone who attends Calvary Fellowship.

This meant we needed to have a two-pronged approach to our outreach. Personal evangelism and invitations to church work well for those who have relationships with people who attend our church. But we found that promotion was our way to reach out to those who do not have any connection with someone who calls Calvary Fellowship home. This meant finding creative ways to let our community know we exist and are here for them. We have used direct mail, billboards, movie theater ads, newspaper ads, and door hangers to get out the word. We usually promote a special event such as Christmas, Easter, or Mother's Day, but we also will promote a series of teachings that we believe will have an appeal to an unchurched person.

What has the result been? In the first eighteen months of our church, we saw no one come to know Christ in our church; in the last eighteen months, we have seen over seven hundred people make a first-time decision to follow Jesus. My point is that for things to change, we had to change. My hope is that you think through your evangelism strategy and look for new ways to get the greatest news ever known to man out, so more can come to know Jesus.

CHAPTER 32
Your Main Evangelistic Engine

Your weekend services are the biggest front door to your church. They are also the biggest factor for whether they make a decision to follow Jesus at your church or not and if they stay at the church at all. The level of excellence in which you execute your weekend services is largely based on your response to this statement: Your weekend services are the most important event in your community. Parades don't matter as much, association meetings don't matter as much, and PTA gatherings don't matter as much. The most important hour in your community is what happens in your church on Sunday mornings. Now, are you executing your weekend services in light of that reality? The reason why some churches have very poor Sunday services is that they have forgotten the power of the Word of God and the feeling of joy over one changed life.

When a church doesn't start on time, it sends a message to everyone there. It says, "We have no idea what we're doing.

We had all week to prepare for this service, but we didn't do it." Here's something I learned a long time ago: No one gets excited over mediocrity. You've never hurried to call your friend to tell her that you just had the most "OK" BLT ever. In fact, "OK" is, to quote Simon Cowell, "It's not terrible. It's just forgettable." Mediocre isn't going to cut it if you want to reach people with the Gospel. The word Gospel doesn't mean "Decent News, OK News, or Not Bad News!" It means Good News! That's the message that we are communicating every Sunday.

Think about the power of Sunday. Where else can you have the undivided attention of a group of people for an hour? Television can't do it. They have to pepper in commercials to pay the bills. If sporting events could do it, they would do away with halftime and just keep going. When a church grabs hold of the notion that their Sunday service is the most important hour in their city, everything changes. The preaching becomes clearer and more concise. The music becomes better and more passionate. The attitude of the church goes from humdrum to happy. The congregation stop checking out halfway through the message and, instead, start inviting their friends to check out their church.

Yet, this change of heart begins with the leaders of the church. It begins with planning services and talking through the implementation of each movement of the service. It moves to the major players of the weekend services as they design their elements to highlight the focus of the service. It trickles down to every volunteer who learns the battle cry that "The message begins in the parking lot" as they see what they do as connected to what the pastor does when he stands to preach the Gospel. But it all begins with answering one question: Do you believe your Sunday service is the most important hour of the week in your community?

CHAPTER 33
How to Promote your Church

It has been said that Las Vegas has nothing to say, but they know how to say it. As the church, we have the most important message in the world, and we struggle to find the right way to share it. The challenge for the church is huge: How do we get a fast-paced world to slow down and hear the message that has the power to change their lives? One way is through the promotion we use to get the word out about our church. I have found that effective promotion does all of the following four things:

Effective Promotion Avoids "Churchy" Language

I recently had a flyer on my door that said, "Are you sick of being told a feel good message? Do you want to hear about being washed in the blood of the Lamb? Do you want to know about being justified in the Spirit? Do you want to feel the power of the Holy Ghost? If so, then come to _____ Church where all visitors are welcome." Forgive me for sounding critical, but no one without a theology degree is going to be able to decipher that message, much less an unchurched person on my block. Too many times, we feel everyone talks "the language of Zion" simply because we are only around other Christians. The reality is that most people have no idea what any of the language on that flyer means.

Someone was in our church office recently, I used the term "the Lord's Day", and they thought I was talking about Christmas rather than Sunday. If we are going to promote the message of the Gospel or the existence of our church, we need to do it in a way that unchurched people will understand.

Effective Promotion Tells People the Benefits

If you send a postcard to your community inviting them to your church, what can they expect? Whatever it is, make it clear on the piece of mail you're sending them. Too many times, churches don't let people know what the benefits are of the program, ministry, event, or service to which you are inviting them. If you are doing a series of messages on parenting or are giving a seminar for engaged couples and you want unchurched people to come, tell them how they would benefit from attending. If following these principles could transform their relationship with their children, say that. If learning the skills in this seminar will greatly improve their chances for a successful marriage, communicate that. People want to know what the benefit will be if they decide to attend. Don't keep them wondering; tell them.

Effective Promotion Removes Fear

People are generally fearful when walking into an environment that is unknown to them. In this area, I believe churches that meet in rented facilities have an advantage over churches that have their own buildings. If you meet in a school or a movie theater, chances are the average person in your community has been inside that facility for one reason or another. If you own a church building, it's possible that they have never even noticed your facility, much less been inside it. Removing fear is about explaining what they will experience if they attend. Telling someone how long the services are is one way to remove fear. Letting people know to "come as they are" is another way to make them feel at ease. The point is, the more barriers you remove, the more likely it is that people will attend.

Effective Promotion Creates Interest

We recently did a series through the Song of Solomon and taught on the subject of sex and relationships. We purchased a billboard, and everyone from Channel 6 and Channel 10 to the *Miami Herald* showed up to cover the story. They were astonished that a church was talking about sex. I knew it was an important topic for our church, but also that it was an area of interest for our community. So, while "The Song of Solomon" might not grab the attention of people going down the 826 expressway in Miami, a billboard that says "The Naked Truth about Sex" will probably get more than one head to turn. The point is to communicate in a language an unchurched person understands.

The best part of promotion from a church perspective is that we aren't alone. God is working in the lives of people before they even receive a piece of mail, see a billboard, or hear a radio ad. Promotion is about us collaborating with God to see as many people as possible to come to know Jesus. So, don't leave this avenue as an unused tool at the bottom of your toolbox. Use it, and see how effective it can be in your ministry.

CHAPTER 34
Money Matters

"Money isn't everything, but it's right up there with oxygen."
—Zig Zigler

When I started Calvary Fellowship, we had no money, no members, and no facility to meet in. The first night we met, the offering was $25. It was at moment that I realized the role money played in a successful church. Truth be told, I was afraid to talk about money. I have such distain for the shenanigans I see on TV, that I swore I would never be like those preachers. Instead, I did the exact opposite: I never talked about money.

In the first three years of our church, I spoke on the subject of money once. You may want to read that sentence again. One time. That's it. Of course, that one time I spoke on money, I apologized for talking about it the entire message.

I went to the office the next day, and one of our pastors asked if he could speak with me. He came into my office and asked if tithing and sacrificial giving played an important role in my life. I said that yes, giving was an important part of my life, and I would never stop tithing because I have seen the blessings of God in my life over and again. Then, he delivered the deathblow. He said, "If giving means so much to you, and it's such a blessing, why do you rob our church of the same blessing by not talking about it?" I was floored. I had never thought of it that way. I was so concerned with how a few disgruntled Christians would see me that I never even considered what the majority of the church was missing. So, what I share with you in this chapter are lessons learned the hard way.

A Theology of Stewardship

Many pastors have never studied the subject of money. Because stewardship is rarely studied in seminary or Bible college, most pastors know very little about money management, investing, cash flow, or budgeting. I believe every pastor should become an expert in financial areas because the health of your church depends on it. If you don't believe me, talk to a church planter or pastor who has closed his doors. Ask him to give you five reasons why they closed. I can promise you lack of funding will be on the list.

The best book I have ever read on the subject of stewardship is Money, Possessions, and Eternity by Randy Alcorn. I would encourage you to study this book and others like it to gain a solid understanding of stewardship. This way you will be able to lead your church with confidence in financial matters.

Your Giving Affects the Entire Church

When God isn't blessing a church financially, there are a few places to look for the cause. The stewardship system in the church is the most obvious place to look. A bad system will produce bad results. If the system is sound, then it's time to look deeper. We must look at the giving of the key leaders in the church. When a pastor isn't tithing, God's hand of blessing is removed. When staff members aren't tithing, God will many times slow down the blessing, so pastors can take note of it. Pastors, staff members, and leaders need to be tithing for the full blessing of God to be realized. God promises to "open the windows of heaven" to the person who honors God in tithing. Too often, the lack of resources is rooted here. God allows this to take place so leaders will deal with this issue of non-giving. Here is my personal philosophy: Non-tithing staff members need to be released. Their lack of giving shows their lack of maturity and disregard for the church's mission. Like Achan in the book of Joshua, the sin needs to be removed from the camp for God's blessing to return.

Model a Debt-free Lifestyle

One of the greatest freedoms in life is financial freedom. I remember being in debt. I remember the pressure, the frustration, and the pain. I felt pressure because I was spending more than I was making, and eventually, I had to pay the piper. I felt frustration because my poor stewardship forced me to say no to great opportunities. I felt pain because paying it all back hurts a lot more than spending it. But I also remember the day I mailed in my last credit card payment. It was glorious. I was officially debt-free. I don't know if I've ever been happier. I openly share my story when I speak because I need to model a debt-free lifestyle to my church.

Model Generosity

Andy Stanley calls this being a "progressive giver." That is, we increase our giving each year. Too many Christians start tithing, and that's where their giving stays forever. To be a progressive giver means to increase your percentage of giving above the tithe. As a pastor, you may not be the top giver in your church. However, I believe no one should be giving more sacrificially than you should. I believe this is a key to God's blessing. God blesses leaders who can be trusted.

So, make a decision to be an expert in Biblical stewardship. The more you grow in wisdom and knowledge of stewardship, the more God is able to bless you and your church. You can take that to the bank.

CHAPTER 35
Make It Easy for People to Give

Do you remember the old days when church was simple? I don't, but I've heard it was simple. People would come to church and put cash in the offering, and that's how everyone gave. Then, checks entered the scene. Later, credit cards became a normal part of our lives. Now, we get asked about automatic deductions and paying for services on a company Web site amidst a host of other ways to transact in this economy. How has the church responded? We're still only receiving the offering on Sunday morning, hoping it's enough to cover all of the church's needs and be able to fund the church's vision. I contend that to have only one means of receiving tithes and offerings is a mistake. Instead, I encourage you to take the approach of making it easy for people to give.

Many churches have multiple services, so it's easy for people to attend. Many will open extra parking, so it's easy for people to park. Yet, when it comes to giving, we receive Sunday's offering, and that's the only opportunity people have to give. I believe we do people an injustice and handcuff the church by only having one opportunity to give. One of the secrets to having an effective stewardship system is making it easy for people to give. Here are a few opportunities you can make available to your church:

The Sunday Services

If you want people to be more likely to give on Sunday, put an offering envelope in the bulletin. This way, people feel as though that envelope belongs to them. Some churches put them on the back of the chair or pew. This tends to be less effective because the average person believes those envelopes and everything else on the back of the pew belongs to the church. If you will take the time in your service to receive an offering, people are more likely to give.

The Envelope

One of things we've done is make our offering envelope a business reply envelope, so if people aren't prepared to give on Sunday, they can take the envelope home, place their check inside, and send it in without having to find a stamp. This has been an incredibly effective tool. The reason being, it gives us an opportunity to mention it during our weekend services. We like to say, if they take the envelope and put a check inside, all they have to add is the saliva to seal it, and we'll take care of the rest.

Online Giving

We live in an electronic world. It is not only important for the church to have a Web presence, but also to give people the opportunity to give online. Companies such as Paypal have made setting up an online giving account very easy. This way, even if people are out of town, or they forgot to give, they can log on and give their offering.

Online Banking

Long gone are the days when it was commonplace for people to take their checkbooks with them everywhere. Instead, most people are paying their bills electronically. We encourage people in our membership class and throughout the year to add the church as a regular payee on their online banking, so they can tithe online the same way they pay their power or water bill.

Auto-debit

Most of us have received information from our insurance company, phone company, or the bank financing our car payment that we can have our monthly payment automatically deducted from our checking account simply by filling out a form. We took that idea and created our own form where a person could authorize us to deduct a certain amount each week or each month. This has been incredibly effective for us, as people know they are being obedient in their giving. This also happens to be the method that most of our staff uses. What I love about this method is that it creates consistency in your budget.

Here's the bottom line: Make it easy for people to give to your church. A church that is difficult to give to will not be a well-resourced church. Think through your systems, and create opportunities for people to give. Your mission is too important to let finances stop you from succeeding.

CHAPTER 36
Supersizing Your Small Groups

I am a firm believer that Sunday morning is the rudder that steers the church. However, I also know that Small Groups are the glue that hold a church together and are the engine that develops new leaders. I came out of a culture where there was a ministry for everything from bikers, runners, quilters, bankers, bakers, and candlestick makers. There was also a Small Groups ministry. Despite the size of the church, very few were involved in Small Groups. I wondered why because my experience with Small Groups had been very positive. So, I embarked on a journey when I started Calvary Fellowship to find out how a church can create a culture of Small Groups. What I discovered was that a church with a Small Groups culture utilizes three vital strategies.

Creating a Small Groups Culture

It doesn't matter how important you say Small Groups are. What matters is eliminating the competition to Small Groups. The church that says Small Groups are the focus, but also offers 150 other ministries is confusing people at best and diluting themselves at worst. The best strategy I have seen in creating a culture of Small Groups is to eliminate anything that would stop someone from being involved in a group. We decided to stop our midweek service because we saw people having to choose between midweek and Small Groups. We made it an easy decision by no longer holding midweek services. When people see us hold Small Groups in such high regard that we would rather they be involved in groups than anything else, it begins to create a culture in which groups can thrive.

Maintaining a Small Groups Culture

Many churches begin the process of developing a Small Groups culture by cutting away anything else that would interfere with groups thriving but then fail to go "all the way" to make Small Groups a driving force in the church. What step do they lack? They lack having the entire staff involved in leading groups. Instead, the staff has a pastor whose main responsibility is to oversee Small Groups, and he is the only one who lives, eats, and breathes Small Groups. This is a great formula if your desire is to see 20 percent of your church involved in groups and the other 80 percent involved in one of your other areas of ministry, such as Sunday school or adult education. The opposite approach is to have every staff member leading a group, recruiting group members, and training future leaders. When this occurs, the average person in the church sees the value placed on Small Groups simply by the fact that every staff member is involved in a group. This also keeps the staff connected with people in the church and not locked away in an office for six days and only coming out on Sundays.

Sustaining a Small Groups Culture

There are many factors to sustaining a culture of Small Groups in a church, but I would argue that the greatest factor is that of the senior pastor being the champion of Small Groups. Too many churches never create, maintain, or sustain a culture of Small Groups simply because the champion of groups is a staff member that only speaks once or twice a year to beg for people to open their homes and host a group. Instead, what I have seen in my church, and at every church that sustains a high percentage of people in groups, is a pastor who is committed to doing whatever it takes to see every person in the church experience the power of group life. That means preaching on the importance of Small Groups and modeling it by leading a group each year. When a pastor is engaged in a Small Group, many of his illustrations come from his interaction with those in his group each week. The bottom line is that people don't do what we say. Instead, they do what we model for them.

So, how do you create a culture of Small Groups? In a word, it's focus. When Small Groups are your focus, everything else becomes secondary, and people go where you are leading them.

CHAPTER 37
Facility Matters

We almost started our church in a Kung-Fu studio. I thought it could work, so I took a couple of our future staff members to look at it. I had this vision of greeters standing at the door and saying, "Hi! (Insert karate chop motion here) Welcome to Calvary Fellowship." So, as I gave them a tour, I talked about which way the chairs would face and where the children's ministry would be. As I started to be carried away, they stopped me and said, "Bob, the place smells like feet with a hint of armpit." You see, my sense of smell isn't that acute, so the B.O. that was emanating wasn't getting through to me. However, my colleagues understood something from the very beginning: Facility matters. It doesn't matter if your church owns a building, or you rent a facility, the presentation of your facility is speaking to guests and regular attendees alike.

So what is your facility saying? Is it shouting, "We don't care?" Is it saying, "We are passionate about God and people?"

The best way to find out is two-fold. First, you could ask guests you know who are visiting you for the first time. If I have a friend in town that is coming to our church on a given Sunday, I will tell him, "If you promise to tell me the good, bad, and ugly about your experience with us, I'll buy your lunch." It's amazing how much feedback a free meal can solicit.

The second option is for you or another leader to drive off the property ten minutes before one of your services starts and make your way onto your facility. This way, you are seeing what everyone else sees at the same time he or she sees it. You will see if there's some congestion in the parking lot or some other parking problem. You will notice if your signage is adequate or lacking. You will discover if your building needs to be painted or if the grass hasn't been cut.

Some may ask, "Can't I see if the grass needs to be cut without leaving ten minutes before church starts?" Yes, you can, but you won't be able to see your church from the perspective of a first-time guest without driving in at the same time they do. Most leaders get to church hours before the first service starts and leave long after everyone else has gone home. This is not reality for most people in your community. I can bet there's no traffic jam in your parking lot at 6 AM. There may be one at 10 AM, but most of us don't know that because we aren't ever out there at that time. That's why it's also important to attend your church on weeks you aren't speaking. I like to come to Calvary Fellowship with my family at a particular service and then leave after the service ends, just so I can experience the flow of people in the hallways, determine if the signage inside and outside our building is adequate, and see if volunteers are in the appropriate places.

Wow Factors

Inside your facility, there are several places you can wow people through doing little things. In your restrooms, for example, there doesn't have to be a bad smell. Even though there's a custodial crew that cleans the bathrooms, our team cleans them as well to make sure the bathrooms smell lemony-fresh. In addition, breath mints and lotions always add a wow factor when someone walks into a restroom. Newcomers are generally looking for two places when they walk in—the restrooms and the children's ministry. For that reason, it is important to train volunteers to give helpful directions. This may seem like a small point, but we have all asked for directions from someone working at a movie theater and been given disinterested "it's the third theater on the left" directions. It makes us feel as though we have somehow bothered the person we asked, even though it's his or her job to tell us.

First-time guests don't know the difference between volunteers and staff, so we need to make sure we train staff and volunteers alike to give directions well. At Calvary Fellowship, we have taken a page out of the Disney and Ritz-Carlton handbooks where we don't point people to the children's ministry; we walk them to the children's ministry and let them know about our church along the way. This takes more time and more workers, but guests feel valued when we take the time to walk them to an area personally.

Another wow area is your children's ministry. I have walked into many children's ministries, and my first emotion was fear. I saw two teenagers running a class and thought to myself, "My child isn't a top priority here." Here's the principle: Kids matter. Many times, we say that, but don't do anything to uphold that belief. "Kids matter" means we invest financial, time, and personnel resources to making our children's ministry the best hour of a kid's week. I would encourage you to walk through your children's ministry and ask, "What is this communicating?" If the toys are dirty and old, it's communicating, "We haven't had a baby in our nursery since Carter was president." If there's an inadequate number of volunteers, the message is, "Kids don't matter that much here."

I recently attended a church that meets in a high school, and the message I got when I checked my daughter into the toddler room was, "We've been expecting you." How did I get this message? The toys looked brand new. The volunteers were full of joy and excited to meet my daughter. Once they saw her nametag, they began to call Mia by name. They printed out a name badge for my wife, one for Mia, and even one for our diaper bag, so it wouldn't be confused with someone else's bag. They even handed me a pager like the ones at Outback Steakhouse. They said, "If Mia needs you for any reason, this pager will let you know." The point is that kids mattered to them, and I walked away saying "wow" to myself over and over based on how prepared they were for every child that came through their doors.

In the closets where we store all of our sound equipment, we have a sign that says, "We create environments where guests feel valued." I pray you do the same for your environment and create "wow" moments for every person who decides to attend your church.

CHAPTER 38
Barriers to Baptism

Bottled water has to be the oddest phenomenon in our culture today. There are several different brands, each with its loyal enthusiasts claiming that it's better than the rest. For the record, let me say that I'm a huge fan of bottled water, and the Fiji brand in particular. I take a bottle of it with me wherever I go. A friend recently asked me about why I love Fiji water so much. I could have explained how it has a higher pH that most bottled water, or how human hands have never touched it. Instead, I said, "You just have to try it for yourself to understand."

That's also the case in following Jesus. Perhaps this is why the Bible tells us, "Taste and see that the Lord is good" (Ps. 34:8). That's what we encourage people to do every week in our churches—to take steps and experience God a little more.

Baptism has this idea built into it. As you know, baptism is a command of Jesus. But there's another reason for doing it. In my experience, something wonderful happens in the waters of baptism that cannot be explained, but can only be experienced. I guess in some ways it's like what Morpheus told Neo in *The Matrix:* "No one can be *told* what the Matrix is. You have to see it for yourself."

But what happens when someone's unable or unwilling to take that step into the water? How do we help people overcome the barriers to baptism?

I believe there are four major barriers to baptism. If we understand them, we can help those who've stopped at the edge of the water to move ahead and obey Christ by being baptized.

Lack of Instruction

You preach a message on baptism in which you teach its significance as a command of Jesus, then you invite people to sign up for your next baptism—and the numbers are much higher than your last baptism when you only made an announcement. What's happening here? You're helping people overcome a barrier to baptism without even knowing it.

Lack of instruction about the importance of baptism keeps many people out of the water. There are many in your church who would be baptized if you simply taught on the subject more regularly.

I encourage you to make sure this topic is in your preaching calendar. Also, provide a resource that answers the questions people may have about baptism. At our church, we put a copy of my book *Watermark: An Explanation of Baptism* in the hands of every person deciding to be baptized because we want them to be fully informed of the decision he or she is making.

Tradition

Although I was baptized as an infant, I believe in adult baptism by immersion. In the city I live in, the majority of people were baptized as infants. This is a barrier to adult baptism. Some people say that when you come to Christ, that's when your infant baptism takes effect. I disagree. The Bible says "baptism...now saves you, not by removing dirt from your body, but as a response to God from a clean conscience. It is effective because of the resurrection of Jesus Christ" (1 Pet. 3:20–21, NLT).

How do we help people see the importance of adult baptism in light of their family tradition of infant baptism? My encouragement is not to pit the two against each other. Instead, I regularly tell people, "Your infant baptism spoke of your parents' faith. Now, by being baptized as an adult, you're honoring your parents because their hope when you were baptized as a baby was that you would follow Jesus. This new baptism allows you to make the decision to follow Jesus your own." I don't fight people on the validity of infant baptism. I just encourage them to obey what the Scriptures command.

Opportunity

Many times, people haven't been baptized because we don't offer baptism often enough. I'm not a fan of only a once-a-year baptism event. I know such occasions are exciting and high-energy, but I want to give people the opportunity to obey God now. I don't want to have to tell someone who wants to be baptized, "Great! We'll put you on our list for our next baptism in eleven months." Schedule regular baptisms, so people can experience the joy of obeying God as quickly as possible.

Fear

"I'm not ready to be baptized." I've heard that phrase many times, and it's nearly always rooted in fear. Those who say it are usually afraid they aren't good enough, righteous enough, or holy enough to be baptized. How do we help them overcome this barrier? Our job is to tell them that the only requirement for being baptized is that they've made Jesus their Savior. Perfection isn't a prerequisite. Salvation and willingness to obey Jesus are.

Baptism is what separates the fans of Jesus from the followers of Jesus. It divides those who are merely playing church from those who are serious about spiritual growth and discipleship. It's an important step in the development of every believer. I make no apologies for challenging people to walk into the water. Our role as leaders is to help people become everything God wants them to be. And a big step in their development is baptism.

CHAPTER 39
Membership Matters

Formal membership is something I struggled with early on in my ministry. I felt like the church was different from American Express, where membership has its privileges, so I shied away from any kind of membership process. Instead, I told all attendees they were members of Calvary Fellowship if this was their church home. The results of that decision were disastrous. Interestingly enough, it was not the kind of poor decision making where you see the consequences immediately. Instead, it was a gradual repercussion, like slowly neglecting your health. I believed that a loose definition of membership would not be a detriment to the church, but it most certainly was. The lack of a strong membership process kept the church in a weakened state. Finally, to remedy this, we instituted a formal membership process at the five-year mark of our church's history. The results have been astounding.

Set the Bar High

I have become a firm believer in membership and I am a proponent of setting the bar high as we communicate expectations to potential members. Most churches tend to do the opposite: They set the bar low at membership and then seek to turn up the heat as time goes on. I believe you should turn the heat up from the very beginning because the way a person joins your church is the way they will stay. If you ask for little commitment, I can almost guarantee their commitment will be weak.

We have potential members sign a membership covenant, which states what they are committing to uphold and do as a member of Calvary Fellowship. The covenant involves small group participation, regular church attendance, faithful giving, reaching the unchurched, and serving in the church. We don't apologize for setting a high standard. Instead, we confidently share what the commitment level is and invite those willing to collaborate with us to join.

Keep Members Accountable

A mistake some churches make is that they outline the requirements of membership but never follow up to see if members are following through on their commitment. Leaders who do not follow up on members are doing members a great disservice. Why ask people to sign a covenant saying they will uphold certain values and never check to see if they are doing it? We have found that a review of our members is a great way to discover pastoral care needs in a member's life.

For example, if we see that members haven't been serving in any area of the church for some time, we will call them and ask if something is keeping them from serving. Many times, we will discover a family member who has become ill, has experienced increased pressure at work, or even has a strained marriage relationship. When we have checked the financial giving of members, there have been times when we have seen a member has stopped giving. Once again, a simple phone call can reveal a financial crisis where the church can come alongside and help a family financially or through financial counseling. This tool has greatly helped us in caring for those in our church.

Decide What Commitment Means

Ask any ten people what commitment to a local church means, and you will get ten different responses. Membership has a way of setting the baseline of commitment. If you don't teach what regular church attendance means, everyone will decide for himself or herself. If you don't teach what faithful giving is, people will create definitions of their own. A healthy membership system sets the Biblical standards for the membership criteria and holds members accountable to honor them.

Practical Tips on Membership

One day only. Don't have a membership class that is twelve weeks long. No one is in town that many weeks in a row. Instead, have your membership class in one session. This way, a person can schedule it and get all of the information you want them to know.

Less is more. Think through what potential members need to know and share those things. Trim the fat off your membership class. I believe most membership classes can be reduced to sixty to ninety minutes. Anything more than that, and you may be sharing too much.

What should be taught in a membership class. The history, mission, and vision of your church and the role that each member plays. You can teach the core beliefs of your church (although we teach this elsewhere). Whatever you decide, you must answer the question, "What does a person need to know to make an informed decision to join this church?"

Not everyone will join. The sign of a healthy membership system is that not everyone will join. When your vision is clear, there will be those who aren't going in that direction and will want to find another church to attend. Your membership class exists to explain to potential members who you are as a church. If you do that well, some will decide not to join, but most will join because a clear vision is hard to resist.

Members only. There should be areas of your church where only members can serve. In our church, only members can serve as small group leaders. When a person wants to lead a small group, we check to see if they are members. If they aren't, we sign them up for our next membership class. We believe this is important because we want those in positions that speak into the lives of others to be aligned with the vision and mission of our church.

Removing a member. There will be times when members aren't upholding the membership covenant. There isn't a personal problem keeping them from following through; instead, it is simply rebellion. The course of action to take is to confront them lovingly and ask why they aren't upholding the membership covenant. When they give their reason, ask them to correct it in a specific period. Then let them know you will be following up with them after that period has elapsed. If the members still haven't corrected the situation, contact them again, and let them know that, due to their failure to uphold the membership covenant, you are removing them from the membership roll. They are still welcome to attend the church and, should they resolve this issue, they can reapply for membership.

If you want membership to matter, make it matter. A healthy membership process can make a church even healthier by raising the level of commitment and giving the entire church alignment in its mission. Membership is as important as you make it. So, make it matter.

CHAPTER 40
The Lowdown on Follow-up

It was the best shoe-buying experience ever. I'd gone to Nordstrom's to try on some shoes, and I soon found a pair I couldn't see doing life without. So, I bought them, just as I've bought many other pairs of shoes in my life. What happened three days later blew me away: I got a handwritten letter in the mail from the salesperson, thanking me for my business and including his card for future reference. It was a huge reminder: *Follow-up matters.*

Every Sunday, people come into our churches for the first time. God works in their lives, and many of these first-time guests want to take a step in God's direction. How will we follow up with them? I believe we must trust the Holy Spirit's work in their lives, but I also know we must collaborate with what the Spirit is doing. We need to think through the most effective ways to follow up those in whose lives God is at work.

I believe we should focus our follow-up in the following four areas. While my point for each of these areas isn't necessarily to get you to employ the methods outlined here, it is for you to make sure you have a process in place for following up with people who are making big decisions spiritually.

First-time Guests

Growing churches have a nonthreatening way of identifying first-time guests, plus a noninvasive approach to follow-up that invites them into greater levels of involvement without seeming too pushy. These churches think through ways in how to help first-time guests return as second-time guests, how to encourage second-timers to become regular attendees, and how to motivate regular attendees to become fully committed members.

Salvation

At our church, when people put their faith in Jesus, we follow up by sending a congratulatory e-mail. Then, we mail them a copy of a book I wrote called *Start Here* (go to www.church-resources.com to download a copy of the e-book). It outlines my conversion experience as well as four decisions I made that were vital in my growth as a young Christian. After this, we encourage the people to be baptized and to join a small group.

Stewardship

I give financially to a mission agency that follows up with me every month. They send me a letter indicating how much I gave in the last month, plus my contribution total for the year. They also enclose a letter that tells me how the resources will be used.

However, when the average person gives at a local church, the usual response is silence. What does that silence communicate? It could be communicating a lack of interest. It also creates questions in the mind of the person who gave. People wonder if the church got the check. They ask why they never got a thank you. For many, giving for the first time is a step of faith. We would be remiss not to follow up, thank them for their gift, and let them know how these resources will be used.

Besides sending a thank-you letter when a person gives for the first time, it's also good to acknowledge when a person becomes a tither. (While this is impossible to know for sure without seeing his or her pay stub, I encourage you to set a financial benchmark; then, when someone's giving reaches that amount, it can be considered a tithe.) Reaching this point is an opportunity to send a book or other resource to encourage this person for taking a step of faith and trusting God. In addition, when a person gives a particularly large financial gift, a follow-up phone call or card is very appropriate to thank the individual for their generosity.

Servanthood

We believe that ministry placement is not a life sentence. So, we follow up with servants in our church within the first ninety days of beginning their new ministry role to ask them a series of questions. We give every person who serves the opportunity to say, "I hate this!" Should they dislike their ministry assignment, we place them in a new area and give them a new experience in serving the Lord.

BOB FRANQUIZ

Follow-up is communicating that you care. It gives you an opportunity to be personal in a very impersonal world. My philosophy is if a salesperson is willing to follow up with me over a pair of shoes, I can follow up when someone takes a step in God's direction.

CHAPTER 41
Eliminating "Bored" Meetings

As a rule, I don't like meetings. The reason is that I have spent years of my life in meetings. The majority of those meetings have been a complete waste of time. Then, I planted a church and swore I would never be the cause of one of these "snooze fests." Sure enough, when I became a senior pastor, I committed the same "meeting sins" that those who led me had done. So much so, I even structured my meetings the same way and scheduled them at the same time. As you know, doing the exact same thing and expecting different results is the definition of insanity.

I felt stuck because I knew I needed to meet with staff and communicate with them, but I wanted to know how to do this in a way that was helpful and not deathly boring. What I have learned is that what people dislike about meetings are their length and flow. They are usually slow and boring. So, the solution to this problem is to make them faster and more exciting. This realization helped me create different types of meetings that work to eliminate boredom and increase productivity.

The Staff Meeting

Our staff meetings used to be three hours long and cover every possible subject under the sun. This led to our staff suffering from attention fatigue. It is impossible to stay fresh and engaged for hours on end. So, shortening the length of staff meetings has helped us work through our agenda more quickly and keep a better pace in the meeting. Today, our staff meetings are ninety minutes in length, sometimes shorter. The way we keep it to this length is if someone brings up something that could sidetrack us, we schedule a meeting for that subject.

For example, if someone brings up that our sound system needs to be completely overhauled, this is a meeting that should be separate from the staff meeting. First, we only need the people with expertise in sound in that meeting. If you decide to include the whole staff, you waste a lot of time and money. Second, this long conversation with technical terms will bore most of the staff to tears. This can be handled in thirty to sixty minutes with the right people in the room if everyone is prepared. The important thing is to make sure you don't slow down the flow of your staff meeting.

The Touch Base Meeting

The touch base meeting lasts no more than ten minutes and has one specific agenda in mind. This is not a place to bring up seven things that have been on your mind lately. This meeting is designed to discuss a singular issue and get the team in alignment. Obviously, ten minutes isn't a long time, so I'm not advocating using the touch base meeting to talk about a brand new initiative with your team. However, the touch base meeting is a great type of meeting to use when your production team needs to get a couple of things straight for Sunday's services. I believe most issues can be solved in ten minutes when you have prepared, competent staff.

The Stand Up Meeting

I borrowed the name of this meeting from Patrick Lencioni's book, Death by Meeting. The idea behind this type of meeting is to gather your key people for no more than five minutes to discuss what they will be working on today. If you've ever worked on a construction site, foremen have mastered this meeting. This isn't the time to air your issues or talk about your new vision. This is the time to state what your objectives are today.

I have one of these stand up meetings with my assistant every day I am in the office. I walk in and let her know what my plans are for that day. If my goal is to work on my message for Sunday, then she knows I am "off limits," unless the office is on fire. If I walk in and tell her the times I don't have meetings, she knows she can come in or schedule an appointment for staff to meet with me.

Meetings are important. The key is to give appropriate time and attention to issues that need greater time and not drag out items that can be handled quickly. There is a business axiom that a job will grow to take the time allotted to it. If you give every issue a sixty-minute meeting, then it will take sixty minutes to get anything discussed in your organization. This will lead to staff not being prepared and hours of precious time wasted. When people only have ten to thirty minutes, they come ready for action, and they are prepared to discuss the agenda item.

The mistake I see many organizations make is to cut meetings because they are boring. The solution is not to decrease communication as an organization is growing. On the contrary, we need increased communication, but it must be focused towards specific issues with start and stop times.
So, shake up your meetings by shortening the length and increasing the intensity and watch your productivity go up.

CHAPTER 42
Revisit Important Topics

Imagine a typical South Florida day. Not a cloud in the sky. Ninety degrees with about 100 percent humidity and traffic as far as the eye can see. I was driving to work one such morning, and while sitting at a stoplight, I saw the car in front of mine start to emit an ominous white smoke. I started to think a new Pope was being chosen, but when the light turned green, every car moved except mine. It wasn't the car in front of me acting like a chain smoker; it was mine. What happened? I neglected to change the oil, and the health of my car suffered. I had to replace the entire engine because of my neglect. An oil change costs $20, yet my negligence cost me $1,700. I'm not an investment guru, but I'm sure this was not a good use of money.

Just as there needs to be regular maintenance on your car every three thousand miles, there are also topics that you as a pastor need to return to every twelve months to keep the church healthy. At Calvary Fellowship, we have a list of topics that we add to our preaching calendar every year without fail.

Servanthood

We add messages on servanthood to our preaching calendar for two reasons. First, as a portable church doing multiple weekend services, we need a large pool of servants to make our services happen each week. This includes set-up and tear-down crews, children's ministry, multiple worship teams, and a host of other areas. As the pastor, you are the chief recruiter of new servants in the church. Second, servanthood is a core distinctive of a follower of Jesus. It is the defining characteristic of greatness in the sight of God. "Whoever wants to be great must become a servant" (Matt. 20:26). If we desire to see those in our churches live lives of greatness, then servanthood is the path that leads them there. A healthy church is one where people are serving others for Jesus' sake.

Stewardship

Every Christian is a steward. The question is, "Is he or she a good steward or not?" The Bible says, "Moreover, it is required of stewards that they be found trustworthy" (1 Cor. 4:2). This is a requirement in the kingdom of God. We need to teach on financial stewardship every year for several reasons: First, there are people in our churches who are new and have never heard what God has to say about giving, saving, spending, investing, and debt. We are doing people a disservice by neglecting to teach on this extremely important topic. Secondly, there are people in our churches who need to be reminded of what God has to say about stewardship. Our world is bombarding people with advertisements, sales, and zero-interest balance transfers every day. Teaching on stewardship yearly is not too much. We all need to be taught God's financial principles.

Relationships

If you have many married couples in your church, teach on marriage every year. If you have a large population of singles in your church, then teach on single relationships. I would still teach on marriage in largely single churches; I would just make the series shorter. Singles are very interested in getting married, so the information you share about marriage will have plenty of relevance to them. If your church is like mine (and I'm guessing it is), then you have couples that are struggling in their marriages. Most couples don't know God's purpose for marriage, much less know how to handle conflict or how to communicate. This is why we need to teach these principles every year. Couples who heard last year's marriage series will be happy about the series because chances are they had conflict in the last twelve months and could use the reminder.

Evangelism

This core purpose of the church is the one that, if not focused on regularly, will quickly fade. Most Christians (at least those who don't have evangelism as their primary spiritual gift) need to be reminded that theirs is a lost world, and God has called us to reach them in the power of the Holy Spirit. We uphold the value of evangelism by giving people an opportunity to receive Christ in our services, by creating the kind of Sunday environment where people want to invite their friends, and by giving people the tools to share their faith with those around them. If we say, "People have heard the Great Commission before. I'm sure they get it," we are unintentionally lowering the evangelistic heat in our church. Churches that are white-hot with evangelistic zeal are those that are teaching, modeling, and celebrating evangelism!

Other topics may be very important for your church to teach on each year. The key here is to identify them and make sure they are on the calendar, so our churches don't seemingly "break down" in any area of mission, vision, or ministry.

CHAPTER 43

How to Get Unstuck

Have you ever been stuck? I mean really stuck. We were. Our church started out well and about three years into our history, we flatlined in our growth. We saw new people coming in and just as many people leaving. In fact, I remember the nauseated feeling I had when my executive pastor gave me a spreadsheet of an eighteen-month period in our church where we had growth by only ten people. I don't mean 10 percent; I mean ten individual humans. Some might think I'm being too hard and that I should be happy anyone shows up at all, but I feel called to reach the city of Miami (a city of 2.5 million) and growing by ten people per year and a half. It was going to take me into the twenty-fourth century to accomplish this goal. (Maybe by then, Captain Picard and the rest of the Enterprise crew could help me). I realized that we were stuck, and I knew that, as the leader, it was my job to figure out what was causing us to be flatlined.

That season of my life caused me to develop an eight-point strategy of discovering where I might be stuck. I believe it can help any church leader who must find the place where the church needs tweaks or overhauls for it to reach its full redemptive potential.

Confront Reality

Author Max Dupree says the first job of the leader is to define reality . The problem with leaders is that we are so optimistic, it is hard for us to confront a reality that isn't bright. When I was handed that spreadsheet, I had two options: either tell our executive pastor that his numbers were wrong or deal with the numbers myself. I chose to deal with the numbers. Nothing will happen in your church until you choose to confront reality.

Learn New Skills

Many times, churches are stuck because the leader doesn't feel the need to learn new skills. This is the height of arrogance. We need to be learning new skills continually because we are living in an ever-changing world. Rick Warren is famous for saying, "The day we stop growing, we're dead in the water." There is a myriad of places for us to gain new skills, but it begins with a decision to stop "doing what we're doing" and get serious about our own personal growth.

Get a Coach

One of the best places to get unstuck is through coaching. Coaching has the ability to give us perspective we don't currently possess. First, we get the perspective of another person who is not emotionally attached to our situation and traditions. Secondly, it forces us to get out of our normal routine, and that alone has the ability to give us new ideas and insights.

Find a Model

Models are great—not so we can copy them, but so we can learn from them. When I meet with a leader who is a step or two ahead of me, I always ask how he or she worked through the area in which I might be stuck. This allows me to see how someone else navigated the same problem I am up against.

Check the Gauges

We discussed this in chapter twenty-eight, but I need to be checking the gauges constantly to identify the problem, so I can go to work on it and find a measurable result.

Radical Action

The solution is not just identifying the problem; it is taking action to correct the problem. Too many leaders think talking about the problem fixes the problem. It doesn't. Radical action fixes problems. If your church has been stalled for a year, a slight tweak is probably not going to be the solution. It's probably going to take an overhaul of an entire system of your church to get things on track. The reason why this is radical is that people get comfortable, and when you, as the leader, start shaking things up, it is seen as radical. Radical is good. It's how leaders lead.

Believe in a Better Future

In his book Good to Great, Jim Collins introduced a concept he calls the "Stockdale Paradox," which states a leader must "confront the brutal facts without losing heart." This is at the heart of being unstuck. You must confront reality, but you cannot allow that harsh truth to discourage you from the future God has for you.

Jeremiah 29:11 states, "For I know the plans I have for you," declares the LORD, "plans to prosper you and not to harm you, plans to give you hope and a future." Yet, what makes this passage so amazing is the fact that it is rooted in the middle of a chapter about how the children of Israel would be taken into captivity for seventy years. It is the epitome of harsh reality followed by a belief in a better future. The day the a leader stops believing that the best days of the church are ahead of it, it's game over. Being stuck is part of the story of every church. My encouragement is not to let it become the overarching story of your church. Instead, let the brightness of the future propel you into becoming everything God wants you to be.

PART 4
Personal Development Strategies

CHAPTER 44
Goal Setting

A study was conducted with students in the 1979 Harvard MBA program. The students were asked, "Have you set clear, written goals for your future and made plans to accomplish them?" Of all the students, only 3 percent had written goals and plans; 13 percent had goals, but they were not in writing; and a whopping 84 percent had no specific set goals. Ten years later, the members of the class were interviewed again, and the findings were amazing! The 13 percent of the class who had goals were earning, on average, twice as much as the 84 percent who had no goals at all. And what about the 3 percent who had clear, written goals? They were earning, on average, ten times as much as the other 97 percent put together.[xii] The moral of the story is that goals matter. In fact, I believe goals are the difference between fulfilling the vision God has given you and falling short.

Simply put, goals are dreams with deadlines. Goals force us to think about our future and get specific about what we desire to accomplish. I have a personal rule of setting goals every December for the coming year. These are not resolutions. Everyone knows that resolutions are thrown out with the Christmas tree. The reason many people don't change is that they don't set specific, measurable, and attainable goals that can propel them to where they ultimately desire to be. So, here are three guidelines for setting goals that will serve you well if you follow them:

Be specific about your goals. Too many times, we set goals that are impossible to measure, and thus, we don't know if we've reached them. Here is an ambiguous goal: "To honor God." Honoring God is a worthy endeavor and should be the reason we exist, but how do I know if I'm reaching this goal? A more specific goal might be "I want to invest in my relationship with God by devoting fifteen minutes each day to prayer and Bible reading." While that obviously doesn't cover every aspect of my relationship with God, it is specific and I can look at the clock to see if I am meeting my goal or not.

Is the goal attainable? If you're the pastor of a church of one hundred, don't set a goal that you want to grow to ten thousand attendees in the next six months. I don't say this because I believe it is impossible. Jesus said, "With God all things are possible" (Mark 10:27, NKJV). My encouragement is to set goals that are attainable, but not presumptuous. At the same time, don't set goals that are too low. Stretch yourself, and expect God to work in your life and grow you into the person He wants you to be.

Review your goals. It is not enough to write out goals and file them away in a drawer where they will never see the light of day. I recommend you write out your goals and put them in a place where you can see them. Review your goals weekly, and think through practical steps to achieving your goals.

So, where do you want to be in the next twelve months? Instead of being frustrated every year about how things never change, make goal setting a normal part of your life, and watch how God uses them to transform your life.

Areas of Goal Setting

You can set goals for any part of your life, but I believe everyone should set goals for these six areas:

Spiritual. What is my plan to grow spiritually in the next twelve months? Will I read the Bible in a year? Will I read a devotional book each morning? How much time will I spend in prayer? Will I go on a mission trip to a foreign country?

Personal development. What is my plan to grow as a person this year? How many books will I read? What conferences and seminars will I attend? What hobbies will I take up?

Vocational. How will I grow in my calling and career this year? Will I put myself in environments where leadership is taught, so I can grow? Will I get involved in some form of coaching network to improve my skills?

Relational. How will I improve my marriage this year? Will I spend more time with my children? Will I invest in my friendships more? Where will I go on vacation with my family?

Financial. How will I be a better steward of the resources God has entrusted to me? Will I give more than I did last year? Will I support a missionary? Will I save more? Get out of debt? Will I intentionally invest more into my retirement?

Physical Health: How will I improve my health this year? Do I plan to lose weight? How much weight? By what day do I plan to achieve this goal? How often will I go to the gym? Will I hire a personal trainer? Do I want to stretch myself and run a marathon or participate in a triathlon?

To reach our goals, we have to ask ourselves these important questions. No one has ever reached his or her goals by accident. They are obtained when we are intentional and determined.

Understand the Purpose of Goal Setting

The purpose of goal setting isn't simply to attain the goals you set. The primary purpose of goals is to make us the type of person who can reach these goals. This is the reason I pray and set goals. It is because I want to continue growing as a follower of Jesus and as a leader. Goals have the ability to bring about major growth in my life. Business philosopher Jim Rohn says "Set the kind of goals that will make something of you to achieve them."[xiii]

CHAPTER 45
Effective Time Management

In my study of great leaders whom God is using mightily, I've found several consistent qualities: visionary leadership, a passion for reaching lost people, and an insatiable desire to learn. Another quality I've noticed in these leaders is one that surprised me: Every great leader knows that his time is his life. Time management isn't something that only anal-retentive, noncreative types practice. Every great leader knows that managing your time is the only way to make sure everything you need to accomplish is done.

As a young leader, I focused mostly on the task I was accomplishing and rarely evaluated how much time I spent doing it. Over the years, I've learned that my time is my life, and if I don't manage my time well, I'm not managing my life well.

To help in this area, I've implemented what I call the 4-D approach to time management.

What Gets Done

One of my guiding principles in time management is something I learned from business philosopher Jim Rohn: *Plan your day the night before.* Before I go to bed, I spend a few minutes thinking about tomorrow's most important tasks that I need to accomplish. I make a list, and then organize it by level of importance. This way, I can hit the ground running when I get to the office the next day. I discipline myself to work on the most important items first. Even if that's all I accomplish, I've had a productive day.

What Gets Delegated

Delegation is a required skill for any high-capacity leader, because there's more to do than you can accomplish yourself. This is where we have to focus on our strengths. Ask yourself, "What are the things that only I can do?" If there's something someone else can do, delegate it. Here's the prevailing wisdom: If someone can do it seventy-five percent as well as you, it should be delegated.

Sometimes we think, if it's something I don't like doing, why would anyone else want to do it? However, people around you are waiting for you to let go of certain tasks in their area of gifting and would love to do those things for you. We need to stop robbing people of opportunities to serve.

What Gets Delayed

This category is for low-priority items or tasks that would be nice to accomplish but aren't in your list of top items for that day.

Unfortunately, many times, we delay things that are high-priority because they're difficult. Instead, we should look over our priority items and always do first the thing we want to do least. Brian Tracy calls this practice "eating the frog." If you have to eat a frog today, it's best just to do it first and get it out of the way.

This approach has several benefits. First, eating the frog is probably the worst thing you'll have to do that day; so, once it's done, things can't get any worse.

Second, you free up your mental energy because until you finally eat that frog, you'll be thinking about it and dreading it.

Your frog might be a tough conversation that needs to take place, a hard decision to make, or some demanding project to complete. Whatever it is, do it first—and you'll be happier and more effective.

What Gets Deleted

In his book Getting Things Done, David Allen notes that if he picks up a sheet of paper in his inbox and realizes his life will not change by throwing it away, it is thrown out. This goes along with the rule never to touch a piece of paper more than once. Otherwise, clutter puts our creativity in neutral. This is where we really have to be discerning to know where our time is best spent. I've decided, for example, that most e-mails containing criticism are just not going to get any of my time.

Remember, too, that if you're a leader seeking to make a difference for the kingdom of God, you simply don't have time to waste trying to justify your decisions. I love Nehemiah's reply when his enemies summoned him to come and explain why he was rebuilding Jerusalem's walls: "I am doing a great work, so that I cannot come down" (Neh. 6:3, NKJV).

You and I are involved in the great work of collaborating with God to reach people and change lives. The only way we can affect as many people's eternities as possible is by managing our time well right now.

CHAPTER 46
The "Stop Doing" List

I cut my teeth in ministry in one of the largest churches in America. I am eternally grateful for this experience. However, being on staff at a large church did have one negative side effect for me: It caused me to see my church plant as a small version of a big church. What does that mean? It means we tried to do everything a large church did, simply on a smaller scale. We were less than one year into planting our church, and we had already added men's, women's, singles, Small Groups ministries, and a midweek Bible study. It made sense to me. I had come out of a church that offered options to every attendee, so I figured I needed to do the same in our new church.

I quickly learned that without critical mass and workers to sustain these ministries, they were doomed to fail. We tried to do too much too soon. I was the pastor of a growing church, yet I had secondary ministries that were struggling at best. This meant a very hard decision for me: cut these ministries, so we didn't lose momentum. It was the toughest leadership moment in my young tenure as a senior pastor. We decided to cut everything except small groups, and it has been the best decision we've made in the history of our church. The best way to ensure you don't have to put the brakes on a failing ministry is to learn to say no. What I have learned about myself is that I had a problem saying no. I don't know if I just wanted to be liked, or I didn't want anyone to leave my church, but I started ministries to keep people happy.

Don't Give People False Hope

One of the temptations I used to fight is to hold out false hope for people in their desire to see a ministry begin in our church. "Pastor, do you have a ministry for senior citizens who love to play dominoes in the park?" When I would hear something like that, I would say, "Not yet, but we're thinking about adding a domino ministry in the near future." The truth is, I had never even considered it, but I didn't want to disappoint them.

Why is this a destructive pattern? First, it's not the truth, and lying is never a good thing. Second, it gives people false hope that you are going to start something, and the longer you delay, the more frustrated they become. Lastly, when you don't end up doing what you said you were going to do, you undermine yourself and make it difficult for people to follow you as a leader.

"No" is a Beautiful Word

Today, the scene is quite different. Someone comes up to me and asks, "Pastor, do you have a ministry for people that love shark fishing to the sounds of 1980s heavy metal?" I say, "No, but we have Small Groups in our church where you can grow in your faith and meet other people with whom you may share similar interests." They may ask, "Do you think that a heavy metal loving, shark fishing enthusiast ministry is something you may do in the future?" My response: "No. We have all of our efforts in Small Groups because we believe that people grow best in community, and our Small Groups is where we see that happen most effectively." This may seem simple, but when you're standing in front of a well-meaning person looking to connect with someone who shares his or her interests, it's a harder thing to say. Yet in the end, saying no is best for them and for you.

The best time to stop something is before you start it. Yet, there are times when an area needs to be cut. The challenge for you as a leader is to make the call decisively and then direct people to areas that will give them greater growth and impact in their lives. We say no, not because it's good for us, but because it's best for them and best for the kingdom to have all of our energy pointing in a focused direction.

CHAPTER 47
Learn to Delegate

When Calvary Fellowship got started, I did just about everything. I not only wrote the messages, but I also led worship, printed the bulletins, made copies of the messages onto cassettes, met with every person who needed counseling, set up and broke down the equipment, and handled much of the church's administration. Yet, as time went on and our church began to grow, I felt myself wearing thin due to all of the different responsibilities I was carrying. I felt a bit like Moses who was working his fingers to the bone by himself. When Moses' father-in-law saw this, he asked, "What is this you are doing for the people? Why do you alone sit as judge, while all these people stand around you from morning till evening?" Moses answered him, "Because the people come to me to seek God's will. Whenever they have a dispute, it is brought to me, and I decide between the parties and inform them of God's decrees and laws." Moses' father-in-law replied, "What you are doing is not good.

You and these people who come to you will only wear yourselves out. The work is too heavy for you; you cannot handle it alone." (Ex. 18:14–18).

As I was breaking my back trying to do it all, God brought some amazing people to our church and helped me learn five important principles of delegation:

1. *Being a servant and delegating aren't mutually exclusive.* Servanthood is a core value at our church, and I wanted to model it. The word minister means "under rower," and I wanted to prove that I didn't want or need special treatment. I could set up chairs, type, lift speakers, run cables, and reconcile the church's bank account. What I have since learned is that servanthood is about being servant hearted, not simply doing everything. Servanthood is about believing nothing is beneath you or above you. It is an attitude of the heart where you are willing to do anything for God and His church with joy.

2. *That thing you hate to do, someone else loves to do.* I was amazed to learn that there are tasks I hate to do that others love to do. For instance, I hated designing and printing the church's bulletin. Somehow, the text always ended up either crooked or off-center, as I was getting ready to run copies. Then, God sent a designer who owned a graphic design company, and he asked if he could start making the bulletins. Filled with joy, I readily agreed, and the results were astounding. The bulletin was legible and attractive for the first time in the history of our young church. While making the bulletin was something I put off as last on my To Do list, our

"bulletin guy" couldn't wait to create the program that would be put into the hands of every attendee each Sunday.

3. *Every delegated task needs clear direction.* The greatest error leaders make when they delegate is not giving clear direction to the person being assigned the task. We are so excited to get an item off our To Do list that we give vague instruction as to what we want to see done. When I was overseeing a Bible college as a young leader, I hired an assistant to help me with all the operations of a growing college. I found the best candidate and figured she would simply know what needed to be done. When that didn't happen, I grew incredibly frustrated and started thinking I made the wrong decision. As I reflected on how I had trained my new assistant, I realized my error. I had done very little to communicate my expectations. So, I sat her down and apologized for not communicating clearly. From that day forward, I began verbalizing my expectations and the results were astounding. She blossomed into one of the best assistants I have ever served with, all because I took the time to be clear with the tasks and responsibilities I was giving her.

4. *Every delegated task needs a deadline.* In her book, *If You Want It Done Right, You Don't Have to Do It Yourself,* Donna Genett writes, "Clearly define the time frame within which the task must be completed."[xiv]

Many times, this lack of giving a task without a timeline is the root of much of our frustration. Somehow, we expect people to know what our desire is without ever communicating it. Unless those you serve with have mind-reading abilities, you're going to be required to verbalize your desires. This simple act of saying, "Can you make twenty copies of this packet by Friday at noon?" gives you accountability with your team members. It allows them to fit it into their workload. This way, you aren't hassling them about it every day and should the task not be done within the allotted timeframe, you have an opportunity to work with the person and find out why the task was not accomplished.

5. *Leadership is about creating opportunities to serve.* I used to believe that leadership was about me serving and proving I was willing to do anything. Since then, I have learned that leadership is about focusing on your strengths and creating opportunities for people to serve. The Bible gives us a perfect illustration of this principle:

> In those days when the number of disciples was increasing, the Grecian Jews among them complained against the Hebraic Jews because their widows were being overlooked in the daily distribution of food. So the Twelve gathered all the disciples together and said, "It would not be right for us to neglect the ministry of the word of God in order to wait on tables. Brothers, choose seven men from among you who are known to be full of the Spirit and wisdom. We will turn this responsibility over to them and will give our attention to prayer and the ministry of the word." (Acts 6:1-4)

The apostles were wise beyond their years when they took this course of action. They decided that focusing on their strengths was more important that doing everything themselves. In addition, by focusing on their strengths, they created new opportunities for people to serve and grow in their faith. What was the result of this decision? "So the word of God spread. The number of disciples in Jerusalem increased rapidly, and a large number of priests became obedient to the faith" (Acts 6:7). Proper delegation always leads to increased effectiveness and a win for the entire organization.

CHAPTER 48
From Whom Can You Learn the Most?

I was not much of a reader in high school. In fact, by the time I graduated high school, I had only read one book in my entire life (not including books written by Dr. Seuss or books that were 90 percent pictures). What book was it, you ask. It was an unauthorized biography on the life of Madonna. I bet you never would have pegged me for a Material Girl. Anyway, when I became a Christian, I started to devour books. Then, when I became involved in full-time church work, I started to read at an even more rapid rate. I quickly learned that two types of people write books on the subject of church: theorists and practitioners. Theorists are very smart men and women who research subjects and put their findings into print. Some of these works are very helpful and give us tremendous insight into social trends, cultural changes, philosophical thoughts, and theological insights.

Practitioners are those in the trenches who are leading churches, starting ministries, and leading people day in and day out. They come to us with a wealth of practical insight gained from being in the field. What I am seeing as of late is more theorists writing from the position of practitioners. This can be a problem for leaders who read. While I love much of the material theorists produce on the subject of people sociologically needing to be in community, when they write books on how to start a dynamic Small Groups ministry based on their research, it is potentially dangerous for local church pastors.

One of the mistakes I made early on was reading a book by a theorist and trying to put his finding into practice. While their intentions were well and good, the outcome was disastrous. Why? Quite simply, many of them had never done it themselves. Their views and ideas were simply theories. My rule is, if you haven't done it yourself, don't write a book on how to do it. That's why this book is on the subject of church leadership and not how to become a professional wrestler.

I love to learn from practitioners because what they share is based on experience, and the bulk of that experience has come from the school of hard knocks. One of my greatest joys is to sit at lunch with a leader and ask questions about what they are doing to reach people. I love to listen to men and women in conference settings who are in the trenches engaging in cutting edge, relevant ministry. These people don't have all the answers; they are simply asking the same questions we're asking. The difference is, their experience is producing an answer we can observe, interact with, and modify. Do you want to learn about how a certain model of church works? Pick up the books that many of these pioneering church leaders have written, and learn what you can from them, implement what you believe will help you, and throw out the rest if it doesn't fit your church.

A couple of years ago, I read a book entitled *Watching Baseball* by Jerry Remy, former Boston Red Sox second baseman, who happens to be one of my childhood heroes. The premise of the book is to see "the game within the game" while watching baseball. What made the book compelling to me is that Jerry actually played the game and explains the intensity of America's pastime with the zeal that only someone who played can describe. That's the difference between a theorist and a practitioner. Both have their place, and both can be helpful, but when you want to start a ministry, fix a failing system, or expand your vision, data won't do the trick.

CHAPTER 49

Get a Coach

Tiger Woods has one, and he is the greatest golfer on the planet. Olympic athletes each have one, and they are the finest athletes in the world. Writers have them. Business people have them. People wanting to get healthy get one. What do they have? A coach. Coaching is simply a modern word for discipleship and mentoring. It is where a seasoned leader will invest in the lives of younger leaders and give them insight and training they would have never received otherwise. I talk to many leaders who feel coaching is unnecessary. I believe this decision alone will hinder a leader's ability to lead at a higher level. I firmly believe everyone needs a coach. Many times, people resist coaching because they don't know what it is. Here is a highlight of what coaching is and the benefits associated with being a coach.

Coaching Is not Counseling

I'm a big fan of counseling, but coaching and counseling are not the same thing. Counseling fixes something that's broken in individuals through exploratory sessions that deal with their experience and hurts. Coaching, on the other hand, begins from a place of wholeness, believing that the person being coached is whole and ready to take their church or organization to the next level. If there is anything broken, it is probably a system or structure in the church, and fixing that is the focus.

Coaching is About Thinking Differently

The biggest breakthrough I see in coaching is a change in the way leaders think. Many times, a leader will come into a coaching network, and their church will be stuck. Many times, they believe a cosmetic change will take their ministry to a new level. Yet, as the coaching sessions unfold, they begin to see that a superficial change will not bring about new results. Instead, it is a change of thinking that will take a church to new heights. What do I mean by thinking differently? There is a shift from thinking incrementally to thinking exponentially, from thinking either/or to thinking both/ and, from thinking in reach to focusing outward, and from thinking cosmetic to thinking systemic. These are just a few mental shifts that happen, but the results are extraordinary.

Coaching Is About a New Voice

Many times, leaders are stuck because they don't have anyone to speak into their lives. So, we look at our church only from one vantage point. A good coaching relationship will cause a leader to look at his church from a new perspective and give him insight into how to break through barriers to growth and create systems that will sustain growth.

In my experience as a coach and as someone who has been coached, coaching is about taking your leadership and organization to the next level. Very few can do this alone. Most need someone to come alongside and look at them and their church from an unemotional, unattached perspective. It is here that new possibilities are created and new heights are reached. So, if you want to maximize your church's potential, get a coach.

CHAPTER 50
Help Yourself by Coaching Others

I remember when my mom taught me how to drive. I was fifteen years old and eager to learn because a car meant freedom from the tyranny of asking mom for rides everywhere. Yet, here's what I found interesting: While I was the one learning, she was learning as well. There are laws we forget if we don't get a refresher course now and then. I believe the same is true in church world. My primary calling and passion in life is to pastor my church and see people take their next step towards Jesus. My other world is training and coaching pastors. I believe that if I can influence pastors, I can help them impact their communities through the subsequent actions they take. What I didn't realize is that coaching others made me a better leader. In fact, I learned there are unexpected benefits when we invest in the lives of other leaders:

It Reinforces Truth in Me

Many times, it's through a conversation with a pastor that is asking me questions about Small Groups or hiring staff that I am reminded of the principles that are important to me. All of us can be caught up in the heat of the moment and forget our most basic of guiding principles. When a pastor I am coaching and I are discussing ministry issues in his church, I am learning along with him. I liken it to spring training for professional baseball players. They go through all the basic drills they've been learning since they were playing Little League. They review bunting, turning double plays, and sliding into a base. The Bible puts it this way, "As iron sharpens iron, so one man sharpens another" (Prov. 27:17). Sometimes, we think the only time we learn is when a mentor is speaking to us, but we can be reminded of important truths when we teach others.

It Makes Me More Kingdom Minded

I love leading seminars in my hometown of Miami because it keeps me honest. I'm not just sharing my "trade secrets" out of state, but I am sharing the principles that have helped our church reach people with church leaders right down the street. Doing this takes any hint of competitiveness and crushes it. God is interested in reaching my entire city, and for me to think He is only going to use me to do it, is not only delusional; it's unrealistic. We need all type of churches reaching all types of people.

It Allows God to Bless Me

I believe that when I invest in a leader of another church, God blesses Calvary Fellowship and me. Jesus said, "Freely you have received, freely give" (Matt. 10:8). God hasn't given us experiences simply to help us. God gives us real-life training, so we will share it with others and help them not make the same mistakes we have made. This principle of experience follows the same pattern as finances. God blesses a person with more resources when they choose to give it away and be a conduit of God's blessing. In the same way, God blesses a person or a church that chooses to share what they've learned and give it to others. They operate as a conduit of experience to help other leaders not make the same mistakes.

You may think, "Who am I going to teach? We aren't a large church. I don't have a book out." I started teaching what I knew and helping other pastors when we were a small church. Church planters would call me and ask questions. Bible college students who said they might want to start a church someday would call, and I'd teach them what I knew. We all have unique experiences and unique gifts that qualify us to teach whoever would ask us. Moreover, every time we teach, we end up learning as well.

CHAPTER 51
What Can a Senior Pastor Learn from a Youth Pastor?

Let's be honest, youth pastors are a weird bunch. Conversely, youth pastors say three things about senior pastors drive them crazy. Unfortunately, the piece of paper they wrote those three things on (in crayon) got misplaced. Yet, a senior pastor could learn plenty from the youth pastor on his staff. A great youth pastor shines in relating truth to young people. Youth pastors will go to any extreme and not spare any expense (senior pastors are nodding their heads) to communicate truth in a relevant way. So, as I observe youth pastors do what they do best, I've noted one facet of their ministry in particular that every senior pastor should take note of—their ability to teach youth in a way that results in life change.

Youth Pastors Speak the Language of the Students They Are Reaching...

I recognize that I am a dinosaur at the ripe old age of thirty-five. I tell the students at Calvary Fellowship my age, and they say, "Pastor Bob, you aren't *that* old!" Honestly, I don't really know how to take that. Yet, no matter the age of the youth leader, he knows his mission is to speak the language of students, so they can understand the message he wants them to hear. Every youth pastor knows the language he is speaking will make or break his message. I believe that is why former youth pastors lead many of the most successful pastors in America. Men such as Andy Stanley, Bill Hybels, and Rick Warren all come from youth ministry backgrounds, and they have implemented that model of speaking the language of their audience.

This is so important because so much of America is biblically illiterate. This fact will lead us to do one of two things: It will cause us to insult the culture by saying, "America is going to hell in a hand basket! No one even knows the Ten Commandments anymore." Or, we can understand and engage the culture by saying, "OK, most people don't know the Ten Commandments. What do they know? David Letterman's Top Ten List. Then, let's start there.

The issue here is not watering down the message. The key is to communicate in such a way that people can understand what is being spoken. I have a friend that was in the military. He is one of the top five people in the world when it comes to speaking Morse code. This guy can "Morse" with the best of them. However, my friend isn't working with Morse code any longer.

Why you might ask? It's because no one is speaking Morse code any longer. We have developed different ways to communicate. So, it doesn't matter how wonderful the message is that he preaches with dots and dashes. The only message people can receive and live out is the message that is spoken in a language they understand. Effective missionaries learn this principle. If the people in your audience speak Mandarin, your eloquence in English won't do them any good. We must learn to communicate to our audience in words, pictures, symbols, and phrases with which they can identify.

What does this mean for a senior pastor? It means we have to change our lexicon. The average person does not know what "being washed in the blood means." To a Christian, this is something that is deeply important and full of spiritual meaning and truth, but to an unchurched person, it reminds them of the prom scene from the movie *Carrie*. I am not saying we cannot use these terms when we speak. I am proposing that we define our terms when we use them, so we can accomplish the objective for our communication: understanding and action. This happens when we speak the language of our hearers, and they know what to do. If you don't believe me, ask your youth pastor; he'll tell you I'm right!

CHAPTER 52

Create a Rhythm of Rest

Most leaders find it difficult to rest. One of the reasons for this is that, as leaders, most of us are wired to live off adrenaline, achievement, and anticipating the next step. My wife laughs when we go on vacation because I take more books than clothes. Yet, the reality is that ministry is a marathon, and if I plan to serve God with my whole life, then I have to follow God's prescribed rhythm. What is this rhythm called? The Sabbath—a day where we disengage from our labor and simply live. I will readily admit that it is not easy for me.

When we started Calvary Fellowship, I worked seven days a week for nearly a year. It nearly killed me. I was exhausted, frustrated, and empty. Yet, when I started working in the flow of God's rhythm, I felt energized and happy. What's amazing is that I accomplished more working six days than I did working all seven days.

God instituted the Sabbath as a picture of redemption. He said,

> Observe the Sabbath day by keeping it holy, as the LORD your God has commanded you. Six days you shall labor and do all your work, but the seventh day is a Sabbath to the LORD your God. On it you shall not do any work, neither you, nor your son or daughter, nor your manservant or maidservant, nor your ox, your donkey or any of your animals, nor the alien within your gates, so that your manservant and maidservant may rest, as you do. Remember that you were slaves in Egypt and that the LORD your God brought you out of there with a mighty hand and an outstretched arm. Therefore the LORD your God has commanded you to observe the Sabbath day." (Deut. 5:12–15)

At this time in history, no culture had conceived of the idea to take a day off every week. The children of Israel had been slaves in Egypt and worked without ceasing, so when God told them to take one day off a week, it was earth-shattering. God's plan was for His people to be reminded of His love for them through this gift of rest.

As Christians, the Law of Moses in the strictest sense does not bind us, yet the principle still holds true. Yes, the Bible says that Jesus is our Sabbath rest (Hebrews 4) as He pictures our redemption, but the idea of rest is still an important one. I used to ask myself why God would want His people to take a day off every week. You may be aware of that famous line: The devil doesn't take a day, so why should I?" My philosophy is that I don't want to do anything just because the devil is doing it. At the same time, I believe there are three important reasons to rest a day each week.

You're a Child of God

We tend to think of ourselves by titles. We're husbands, fathers, pastors, sons, brothers, and a host of other designations. While we may be all of those things, we are more. We are children of God. God loves us so much that Jesus died, so we could be His prized possession. It is hard for leaders to think they are loved simply for who they are. You are not a machine who produces sermons. You are not a computer who doles out decisions. You are not a vending machine dishing out Bible verses as remedy for every problem. You are a child of God, and God loves you—not for your labor but for who you are. The Sabbath reminds us of this fact. We are not creating anything, yet God still loves us.

You're not Managing the Universe

A day off also serves the purpose of reminding us that we are not running the universe. If we have to work seven days a week to keep the church running, then something is wrong. We were not created to operate in this way. God uses us because He wants to, not because He needs us. Every time we take a day off, we're telling God that we remember He is in charge—that it's His church and He doesn't need our help running things.

Time to Reflect

The Sabbath also gives us time to reflect on the past and think about the future. Too many times, we're running at such a fast pace that we miss what God desires to speak to us. Yet, in the moments we slow down and change our routine, we hear God's voice clearer.

I'm not advocating that you take every Saturday off in the strictest sense of the Sabbath. I am challenging you to take a day off each week simply to rest and know that the universe is in capable hands and that we are loved by God even when we aren't writing, speaking, counseling, or leading. We are loved simply because we're connected to Him.

CHAPTER 53
How Leaders Refuel

Every effective leader I've ever known has a way of refueling his or her mind, body, and spirit. No person can work continuously without a break, just as no car can function effectively without stopping to refuel. I believe that leaders need to look at *four critical areas of their lives* if they're going to survive the marathon of ministry.

Learning experiences. The old saying is true: "Leaders are readers." I've met very few successful leaders who don't give significant time to reading. The formula for growth is that the rate of the leader's growth determines the rate of the church's growth. So, if I want my church to grow, I have to grow first. That means I need to have a plan for my own personal development as a leader. That needs to include a Bible reading plan, attending conferences that will benefit me as a leader, reading a specific number of books every year, and meeting with other leaders who will stretch my thinking. I also believe that learning from areas outside of our own field helps us be leaders who are more effective. Would attending a seminar on marketing help you be a more effective communicator? Would reading a business book help you look at decision making in a new light? Sometimes, by cross-pollinating our learning experiences, we gain new insight through hearing things from a new perspective.

Your health. A few months ago, I was buying a suit, and as the salesman and I were talking, he asked me what I did for a living. I said I was a pastor (which is usually a conversation killer), and he looked surprised. What he said next shocked me. He said, "I've sold a lot of suits to a lot of pastors, and as pastors go, you're in the best shape of any of them." Now here's what's scary: I was twenty pounds overweight when we had this conversation.

You may be thinking, "Of course, he said that, he was trying to sell you a suit." I'll concede that. Yet, it doesn't change the fact that most pastors are overweight. We have sedentary jobs, people are always offering us food, we work odd hours, and if we were honest, we'd admit that we don't really believe that exercise is that important. We usually quote the verse, "For physical training is of some value, but godliness has value for all things, holding promise for both the present life and the life to come" (1 Tim. 4:8).

Yet, here's the reality: it's hard to do ministry without a body. If you want to serve the Lord for your whole life, you have to get serious about your health, or your latter years of ministry will not be everything they could be. What do I suggest? Join a gym, get a personal trainer, and make sure you work out at least five days a week. It will make all the difference. You'll have more energy, you'll feel better about yourself, and you'll meet people at the gym who are far from God and need the Lord in their lives.

Your family. One of the best ways for leaders to refuel is to spend time with family. After a long day at church, my favorite thing to do is lie on the floor and play with my daughter. We wrestle, color, talk, or dance. It helps me forget about all the stuff that went on at church and allows me just to be a dad and a husband. Vacations help leaders tremendously. By vacation, I don't mean adding a day off to a conference you were planning to attend. I mean just going somewhere with no other agenda than to be with your family.

Every November, my wife and I plan our vacations for the upcoming year. Funny enough, those dates go on the calendar first. If you don't do this, I can promise you that all your time will be filled, and your family will be squeezed out. Instead, with a clean calendar, look at some dates that would work for your family to get away. It will show your family that they are more important than ministry, and you will model the same for your staff and co-workers.

Hobbies. A friend of mine used to say to me, "Bob, your hobby is work. You unwind from work by working more." It was a joke, but it had a lot of truth. I used to think that ministry was a sprint. So, I pushed myself to the limit everyday. Now, being a little older and, hopefully, a little wiser, I've learned that ministry is a marathon and that I need time to myself. I need to pursue interests outside of church because it keeps me sane, and it makes me a more interesting person.

My hobbies are playing guitar and baseball. I'm an avid Red Sox fan and watching a ball game is one of the most relaxing things I do. All I'm thinking about is baseball. Similarly, I've been playing guitar since I was fifteen years old, so whenever I get a chance to plug in and learn to play a new song, it's a great time. Hobbies help us disengage and give us another outlet to meet people beyond the four walls of the church. If you want to know what "normal" people are thinking, go where they are and talk to them.

To be effective ministers, we need to be well rounded in our activities. Focusing on these areas will help us keep our sanity, stay healthy, be stimulated mentally, and remain challenged spiritually.

CHAPTER 54
Create Safeguards

Few events are more devastating to the life of a church than one of its leaders falling into sin. Unfortunately, it's all too common to read a story or watch a news report about another minister who embezzled church funds or ran off with his secretary. I have witnessed the carnage of these actions up close, and suffice it to say, it isn't pretty. Whenever there is financial impropriety or moral failure, it leads to confusion, anger, and a loss of trust in the lives of church members. So, I encourage you to think through two key areas where we need to have the highest integrity in our churches and personal lives.

Have financial systems in place. I was sitting in a meeting years ago with a pastor who told us how a staff member had embezzled millions of dollars over the course of a decade. He challenged me to ask this question, "Is there any way someone could steal money from your church?" This led to the tightening up of the already tight financial safeguards we had in place.

Those safeguards included a spending limit. Although I'm the senior pastor, I have a spending limit. If I am going to spend money that was not approved in our current budget, I have a cap as to how much I can write a check for before needing to consult our board of directors for approval.

A CPA reviews our financial records every quarter. Most churches have a yearly audit. We decided to have a review of our books every quarter.

No one is permitted to count the offering alone. Instead, two people count it and sign off on the amount. Also, we rotate the people who count the offering, so no one counts more than once every six weeks.

We also separate people who have a key to the safe from people who know the combination. If you have a key, you do not know the combination. If you know the combination, you do not have a key. This way it takes two people to open and close the safe.

Have accountability systems in place. No one sets out intending to have an affair and thereby ruining his or her family and ministry. It happens because accountability systems were neglected or never set up. I have four major accountability systems that help me avoid moral disaster:

1. Internet accountability software. I use a great program called Covenant Eyes. This program doesn't block any Web sites. Instead, it records every Web site you visit on a given week and then sends a copy to whomever you decide to be your accountability partner. My weekly report goes to my wife

who sees every site I have surfed. It's easy to say you aren't going to go on any XXX Web sites. It is another thing entirely to know that if you do, the people closest to you are going to find out. There are other similar programs available, but the important thing is to protect yourself from falling into sin.

2. Open door meetings with female staff. My staff is a mix of gifted men and women whom I oversee. This means we all work in close proximity to one another. Yet, I will not meet alone with the door closed with any female staff. Conversely, I will not drive in a car alone with a staff member of the opposite sex. People who fall into sin started out dancing on the line between sin and safety. They get close to the fire, all the while boasting about how they aren't burned. Proverbs 6:27–28 asks us, "Can a man scoop a flame into his lap and not have his clothes catch on fire? Can he walk on hot coals and not blister his feet?" (We need to exercise wisdom and safeguard ourselves from making a mistake that could devastate our churches and families.)

3. No closed door meetings with female church members. I will not, under any circumstances, meet with a woman in our church alone with the door closed. If, on rare occasion, I do meet with a member of the opposite sex, the door is wide open or another staff member is with me in the room. Some find that I am extreme on these issues. Yet, if you talk to leaders who have entered into affairs, a counseling session with a member of the opposite sex is usually where it began. They let their guard down, and the result was disaster. The Bible says, "Your enemy the devil prowls around like

a roaring lion looking for someone to devour" (1 Pet. 5:8). Satan is watching for a moment to pounce and devour us. I simply don't want to give him the chance. Besides, Titus 2:4 says, "Older women should teach younger women." So, I want to make sure that men are meeting with men and women are meeting with women. I believe this is the best way to avoid inviting a lion into your office and life.

In my first year of ministry, I saw the destruction that comes with a pastor falling into sin. My supervisor engaged in an adulterous affair and had to stand in front of the church and confess his sin. Part of me admired his courage to stand before his church family and repent, while many would have run away. Another part of me was so angry with him for letting me down. He was a mentor in my life, and I was deeply hurt by his moral failure.

I remember vividly sitting in the audience the day he stood up and admitted his sin. What shocked me was my reaction. I wept. I prayed a prayer that I have never forgotten and have prayed many times since that night. I prayed, "God, never let me forget this feeling. Never let me forget what sin does. May I stay close to you and take the right precautions so that is never me." I just prayed that prayer again.

CHAPTER 55
Navigating Criticism

"If one person calls you a horse, they're crazy. If five people call you a horse, it's a conspiracy. If twenty people call you a horse, it's time to go out and buy a saddle."

—*Unknown*

If criticism were a spiritual gift, then many would think some Christians were overflowing with the Holy Spirit in their lives. Unfortunately, what is flowing out of the hearts and mouths of many Christians is nowhere near godly. Criticism is a two-edged sword in the life of a leader. On the one hand, a leader who only surrounds himself with "yes men" limits his perspective. On the other hand, the voice of too many critics will leave a pastor wanting to get out of ministry and start flipping burgers for a living. There needs to be a balance where those closest to the leader believe in the vision God has given him, and at the same time, the leader is still able to hear an outside voice that may disagree. I believe to create that delicate balance; *a leader needs to have four factors in place.*

Loyalty publicly. I once heard Andy Stanley say, "Loyalty publicly creates leverage privately." Let's imagine that a staff member disagrees with a decision by the senior pastor (I know I'm talking crazy, but follow me as if it's a science fiction movie). Either the staff member can complain openly, or he can stand by his pastor publicly and then privately share his perspective. What I have learned is that when a staff member shows loyalty to the senior pastor publicly, it garners a heart that is more open privately. The reason is simple: The pastor will know that the person bringing the constructive criticism is loyal to him and has proven it. So, when he or she voices concerns behind closed doors, the pastor feels the information is coming from someone he can trust, even if it's difficult to hear. If you decide to break this rule, and you are disloyal publicly, you lose all credibility in private with the pastor.

The verse. When people walk up to me and begin to criticize me as a leader or Calvary Fellowship as a church, I share one passage of Scripture with them. "But the wisdom that comes from heaven is first of all pure; then peace-loving, considerate, submissive, full of mercy and good fruit, impartial and sincere" (Jam. 3:17). This is the criticism test. When people walk up to me and say God told them to share their "burden" with me, my response is to read this passage to them and see if it passes the test. There are eight characteristics given in this verse. If the person comes with a pure heart and no ulterior motive, is peaceful and not hostile, is considerate in their word choice, has a history of being submissive and not rebellious, speaks with mercy and is not accusatory, has good fruit in his life, is impartial in the sense that he isn't going to profit from this decision, and he speaks with sincerity, then I'm all ears. As you can imagine, few pass this test. Does this mean everything they said was godless? No. However, the lack of these characteristics raises major red flags as I'm listening.

The kernel of truth. Many times, when a person criticizes a leader or the organization he leads, there can be a kernel of truth in what's being spoken. One of the things I have to remind myself of is that some people don't have tact. They follow the motto: say what you mean, and say it mean! While these people can be abrasive and downright annoying, if you can get past the anger and rudeness, there may be something for leaders to learn. This is not easy to do. I believe it is nearly impossible to gain that kernel of truth from only one comment when the person is hostile or abrasive. Yet, if you hear the same criticism repeatedly, even if the messenger can't communicate in a loving way, good leaders try to sift through the chaff to find the kernel of truth.

Create a barrier. For the sake of sanity, all senior pastors should create a barrier between critics and them. I am not advocating isolation, but I am encouraging wisdom in deciding who gets your time. It is impossible for a pastor to meet with everyone who requests an appointment. Due to this reality, pastors need to be selective and spend time with those who will yield the greatest impact. While it may be tempting to meet with every complainer, so you can try to justify your actions, you will quickly find this to be an exercise in futility. Complainers don't stop complaining with explanation; they simply look for something else to complain about. Argumentative people are always looking for arguments. My solution to this problem has been for other people to deal with these people. If they bring up a valid concern, my staff will bring it to me. It's not a perfect system, but it will help you keep your sanity.

I believe it is unhealthy for pastors to listen to negativity continually. This issue is what wears pastors down and eventually leads many ministers to leave ministry altogether. Instead, surround yourself with people who believe in you, who believe in what God has called you to, and who are loyal to you as a leader. If a criticism has merit, it will make its way through the ranks and get to the appropriate channels. If not, then those with the "gift of criticism" may need to find another church, and you can rejoice (in secret, of course).

CHAPTER 56
Don't Be Afraid to Challenge People

I have a friend who was in the military. When I say he was in the military, he wasn't just an average soldier. He was an Army Ranger. He was also part of a Special Forces unit. One day, he and I were driving to lunch, and I asked him, "What possessed you to join the Army and be part of this special unit?" Without missing a beat, he said, "Because they offered me a chance to be the best. They challenged me to either be the best or go home." It was at that moment that I realized when you challenge people, you invite them to go to a higher level.

Too many times in the church, we shy away from challenging people because we don't want to offend. Truth be told, the only people who get offended when we lay out a challenge are people who don't want to grow. I have learned that people are looking to be challenged. They are looking for something to which to give their lives. They are seeking to become more than they currently are. The church can be that place. But for that to happen, pastors need to step up to the plate and become comfortable about challenging people.

Challenge People to Care

The only way people are going to grow spiritually is if they care about growing spiritually. This means putting in the time, effort, energy, and discipline necessary to grow. Is spiritual growth easy? No, it isn't. There's a reason half-hearted people don't become spiritual giants. Jesus said that the call to discipleship is a call to lose your life. That's total commitment. If we challenge people to care and show them the benefits of obedience (i.e., pleasing God, making a difference for eternity, and being who they were created to be), people will respond.

Challenge People to Push Themselves

We recently taught a series through the New Testament, and we challenged people to attend every week of the twelve-week series, attend a Small Group, read a daily devotional, and read the entire New Testament in two months. We made no apologies. We laid out the challenge, and we watched God work in people's lives as they took steps in God's direction. We challenged people in this series to give, serve, extend forgiveness, and love the unlovable. The response was overwhelming. We said at the outset, "If you take this challenge, you will grow more in the next two months than you have in the last two years." We were right, because challenges always bring growth.

Challenge People to Live by Faith

I used to be scared to challenge people to give financially. I didn't want to be misunderstood. Today, I challenge non-givers to begin tithing, and I challenge tithers to start giving generously above the tithe. The underlying motive is a challenge for people to live by faith. The Bible says, "Without faith it is impossible to please God" (Heb. 11:6). Yet, at times, we try to present a belief system that lives apart from faith. If we don't challenge people to live by faith, then their ability to grow disappears. You've probably heard the expression that faith is like a muscle. For faith to grow, it has to be put under pressure. I've learned that making Christianity easy for people isn't Christianity. It's like imitation crabmeat. It might look like it and smell like it, but at its core, it's fake. Christianity is about constantly trusting Jesus more. It's about walking where He is leading and releasing control to Him. Christian leadership is challenging people to take their next step towards Jesus.

Push vs. Pull

There is a difference between challenging people and pushing people. We don't push people to do anything. Instead, I believe to challenge someone is to pull them to somewhere new. If you've ever encountered a door, then you know pushing and pulling aren't the same things. Pushing someone involves moving him or her to a place you haven't been yet. Pulling, on the other hand, begins with your standing where you hope the other person will stand as well. Pulling says, "I've experienced this myself, and it's made all the difference. Join me." We pull by issuing the challenges of Scripture and inviting people to "taste and see that the Lord is good."

CHAPTER 57
Church Hoppers

One of the mistakes pastors make is the decision to fish in the small pond. Here's how it works: A pastor comes to town to plant a church, and the first thing he does is try to reach people who are already attending other churches. This is a huge mistake. Why? It's because the pool of people attending church is much smaller than the pool of people with no connection to church at all. In Miami, over 90 percent of people have no connection to a church whatsoever. So, why would I try to focus on the few that are already attending somewhere? It doesn't make sense. The reason pastors do this is that they believe it's easier to reach other Christians than it is to reach lost people. While having Christians attend your church can be a blessing, there are also dangers in reaching Christians, specifically church hoppers. In fact, if you've attracted a church hopper or two to your church, here are *ten phrases they love to use:*

"But my old church..." This is one of the classic lines of church-transfer Christians. This is where they want to turn your church into their old church. Every time I hear this line, my response is, "If you liked your old church so much, why didn't you stay there?" They usually respond, "Because the church was dead, and your church is alive." This is where you need some backbone, because what you need to say is, "If we start doing what your old church did, we'll become as dead as them." Don't be pressured into turning your church into someone else's church. It's not healthy and not right. God gave you a vision. Be obedient to what God has called you to, not what someone wants to turn you into.

"I just need time to get fed." This is church-speak for "I don't want to do anything. I'm here just to sit and see what I can get out of this church, so don't expect me to serve in any way, shape, or form." This is one of the characteristics of churches that reach mostly Christians from other churches: the congregation doesn't serve. New Christians want to serve. They are excited about what God is doing in their lives. Church hoppers love to just sit and evaluate.

"I'm looking for a church that teaches the Word." This usually means "I'm looking for a church that dispenses lots of information without challenging me to do anything." Translation: "I want you to teach on subjects that tickle my curiosity." Don't let the whims of these people deter you from teaching what you feel God is leading you to teach.

"We came here because we were looking for deep teaching." This is the close cousin to the previous statement. The issue here

is that their last church focused too much on actually obeying the Word. So, they're looking for a church that just talks about the Rapture, the Second Coming, who the Hittites were, and the identity of Theophilus.

"I should know my pastor." This means, "In my last church, I got to know the pastor, but when the church grew, and the pastor couldn't have dinner with us every Tuesday night, I left and came here." The truth is, not everyone in your church needs to know the pastor. They should be able to have their needs met and grow in their faith and in relationship to others in the church, but a personal relationship with the pastor or another staff member is an unrealistic expectation.

"We want a church that's focused on discipling people." At first, this sounds good because, after all, what pastor worth his salt doesn't want to lead a church that's focused on discipleship. Yet, when you dig below the surface, what they mean is, "I want a church that's focused on me, not people who are lost." This kind of mentality kills the evangelistic fervor of a church. Discipleship is about helping live out the faith and be obedient to the Word of God. Discipleship is not simply the acquiring of knowledge. Unfortunately, many times, the people who have the most knowledge about the Bible obey it the least.

"I wish you wouldn't focus so much on what people need to do." This means the church hopper is annoyed that you are calling people to commitment. I've been accused of telling people they need to work for their salvation because I challenge people to live out the truths of the Scriptures. I believe salvation is a gift, but I also believe that a follower of Jesus should be seeking

to grow and become more obedient to God. Yet, when you don't want to grow, any kind of challenge to obedience is convicting, and the response is either repentance and obedience or blaming and complaining. Unfortunately, many Christians choose the latter.

"I wish you wouldn't talk about money." Translation: "I didn't give in my old church, and I'm not going to give here, so please move on." In my experience, people who tithe faithfully enjoy messages on giving: first, because they are reminded of God's promises to those who honor Him with their finances; secondly, because they want others to experience the blessing of trusting God and giving. Church hoppers don't want to hear about giving because it convicts them, and they don't want to change. After all, why do you think they left their last church?

"My old church/pastor was..." Here's a promise I can make you: The way people come into your church is the way they will leave. If they showed up speaking ill of their old church or pastor, they will leave saying the same about you. When I was young in ministry, I would listen to this slander and believe their false praise of our church. Unfortunately, a few scars later, I learned my lesson. If someone comes to your church and says that the teaching was weak at their old church, they will leave saying the same thing about you.

"Pastor, I've been talking to a lot of people and they all say..." I used to fall into this trap. Here's how I've changed: Today, I say, "Who are the people? What are their names?" The church hopper's response is usually something about confidentiality. I always respond, "I want to thank these people for their

suggestion. What are their names?" When they still won't tell me (they never do), I say, "Here's what I believe: you haven't talked to ten people. You've talked to one person ten times." People know there's strength in numbers, so they fabricate numbers to bolster their agenda. If there's a problem, I can promise you that you'll hear about it from several sources if you keep your ear to the ground, ask good questions, and if you are known as someone who is seeking to improve.

    A chapter like this can seem like I don't like Christians. I love Christians. I'm going to spend all eternity with them, so I'd better get used to them. Some of the most faithful volunteers we have are people who came to us from other churches. So, just because people attended a church previously doesn't make them church hoppers. My warning is to be careful you don't lose your focus because of the demands of people who are going to leave your church once they hear there's a new show in town. If someone attends your church and falls in love with the vision of the ministry, great. If they show up and use one of these ten phrases, then to quote a famous movie: "Run, Forrest, run!"

CHAPTER 58
The World's Most Awkward Conversation

How do you ask someone to leave your church? No matter where you are in your ministry, at some point, it will have to be done. Unfortunately, there's no manual on how to do it outside of a few Bible verses. Few authors write about it, so most of us are left in the dark on how to do the one thing no pastor ever thinks he's going to have to do. Call it arrogance or ignorance, but I never thought I'd ever have to ask someone to leave our church. I assumed that all people would have the joy of the Lord in their hearts and a kingdom agenda in their minds.

To say I was wrong would be a gross understatement. I've had more of these awkward conversations than I'd care to admit, but I will say that every time I have one of these meetings, I leave more convinced about who we are as a church, and I've never regretted the decision. That doesn't mean I enjoy these talks. In fact, I hate them. I'm not even sure what to call them. Is it disfellowshipping? Is it church discipline? Or is it just "giving someone the boot"? It's probably all of them, but for our purposes, we'll call it asking someone to leave our church. I can't say I've learned everything about these conversations, but I do believe I have learned some principles for doing this in a God-honoring way. So here are my ten rules for asking someone to leave your church:

The final conversation shouldn't be the first conversation. When you decide that someone needs to leave your church and find another place to worship, your meeting with him or her should not be the first conversation that a staff member has with the person. There should have been a series of conversations before this one. Is this cumbersome? Yes, it is. But the last thing that should be said of you is that you are "trigger happy" about kicking people out of your church. One of the points you need to bring up is that two, three, or four other conversations have led to this. To avoid due process will hurt your church in the end because people will find out you've asked someone to leave.

Document everything. There's an old saying that says, "The shortest pencil is better than the longest memory." That certainly applies here. Document every phone conversation, personal confrontation, and meeting a staff member or leader has with the individual. There's confidence when you walk into a meeting with a file that has every meeting, infraction, and action that the church has taken with this person. Make sure you've reviewed this file and talked to the appropriate parties who have had contact with the individual. You don't want to walk into this meeting and be blindsided with new information about a conversation you know nothing about.

Handle it biblically. You should review every passage on church discipline before entering the meeting. You may have these passages memorized, but you need to read 1 Corinthians 5 and Matthew 18 before these meetings. It opens your heart before God and gives Him an opportunity to speak into our lives. Also, don't allow this to become a gossip session. Too many times, people in our churches will tell us when someone is sinning. That's fine, but they need to go to the person first. If they won't listen, take someone else. If that doesn't work, call the elders (Matthew 18). We need to make sure we're handling these situations biblically. I'm amazed at how people will sin as if it's going out of style, yet get bent out of shape over our approach if it's not in the Matthew 18 order. We need to be above reproach in these matters. So, even if they aren't honoring God, let's make sure we are by following the appropriate, biblical steps.

See this as a last resort. This is not a method to get rid of all the people that bother you from the church. This is last resort when you believe there's no hope here, but to "turn the person over to Satan" (1 Cor. 5). As pastors, we are shepherds. This means we need to be patient with people and bear with people's faults. It is only when we see people beginning to hurt those around them that we must act decisively, out of love for the rest of the church.

Get wise counsel. If you are going to be the one who meets with these individuals and asks them to leave, ask other pastors in the church for their wisdom on the situation. I am looking for any hope that these people may change. However, if I get counsel that this situation isn't going to get better, I act. Getting counsel also helps me not get emotional about the situation. I am able to stay calm and get the facts before I meet with the person being asked to leave.

Have someone with you. Do not meet, under any circumstances, with the person alone. You want to have another person, preferably another staff member, with you to be witness to how the meeting transpired. I personally prefer public places. A coffee shop near my office has seen many bad meetings over the years. I can't even walk in without getting a stomachache. Make sure the person with you is taking notes. This way, after the meeting, you have a complete file on the person from start to finish. You never know when you're going to need it.

Keep it short. These meetings can drag on for hours if you allow them. This meeting should be no longer than thirty minutes. It could be as quick as five minutes, but people want to be heard, and it's important to allow people to feel as though they've said their piece. Don't make a bunch of small talk before the meeting. This is a serious meeting. Pray before you begin, and then tell them why you've asked to meet with them. State the facts, and then let them know they are no longer welcome at your church. Answer the questions that arise. Hear the person out if they have a counterpoint. However, once that's done, repeat the facts, and let them know they are no longer welcome at your church. Don't argue doctrine, philosophy of ministry, or anything else. Inform them of your decision, and that's it.

Pray a prayer of blessing on the person. I always end the meeting by praying a prayer of blessing on the person that's leaving. The person has sinned, but God still loves him. My prayer is that this situation would be a wake-up call for repentance. I pray for God to reveal Himself to the person as he takes steps of obedience and turns from the wickedness. Let him know that while he is not welcome at your church, he should repent of his sin and find a church where he can grow. I don't hate anyone I've asked to leave. In fact, I have found that in the days and weeks after asking them to leave, I pray for them often. I wish them nothing but blessing as they turn from sin and turn to God.

Leave room for repentance. I will be honest, I have never had a person burst into tears and repent at one of these final meetings. What I have witnessed is plenty of pride, blame shifting, and hard hearts. I have always prayed before these meetings that I wouldn't "quench a smoking flax." If the person repents sincerely, I will accept it and work with him. I am yet to see it in all my years of ministry, but I would give a truly repentant person grace if I saw it.

Be honest but not slanderous. The news of these meetings spreads faster than a Southern California wildfire. People may ask what happened at the meeting. After the meeting, people asked to leave will call everyone they know in the church and tell their side of the story. People will ask for our side of the story and try to sort it out in their minds. I used to say nothing. I think this is a mistake. I believe you should be honest, but you don't have to be specific. You could say, "We did have a meeting with _____, and he was asked to leave the church. This is not a decision that came about overnight. We met with him fives times and tried to get him on the right track, yet we saw no repentance. Each time, he refused and continued in his sinful ways. There comes a point in time where you have to let someone go and let God work in his or her lives. I just couldn't allow him to stay and hurt other people in the church. I would not be a faithful pastor if I allowed one person to hurt dozens." This allows you to answer the question and be honest without divulging details no one else needs to know.

If you're going to be a leader, then at some point, you're going to have one of these conversations. These meetings go about as well as a root canal; it's not pleasant, but if done right, they remove a problem, and the church is healthier because of it. My hope is that you follow these steps and stay above reproach in these matters, so you can lead your church at a higher level.

CHAPTER 59
Ten Questions Leaders Should Ask Themselves

One of the things that separate average leaders from above average leaders are the questions they ask themselves. When average leaders do ask themselves any questions, they're usually vague questions that can't be quantified. "How are things going?" is too vague to give us good data. In contrast, an above average leader would ask, "In comparison to this week last year, what percentage of people in our church has been baptized?" Two questions, yet worlds apart. To be an above average leader, there are questions our leaders should be regularly asking themselves. Here are ten that I ask myself at least once a quarter:

"If my church disappeared, would it matter?" I learned this question from a friend of mine who was struggling with the answer. He had evaluated his area and found a number of churches similar to his. Upon further research, he learned that many of those in his church came from one of these churches and that very few people were coming to faith in Jesus at his

church. He concluded that if his church disappeared, it wouldn't matter, since his church was a carbon copy of the churches around him. To say this is a hard pill to swallow would be an understatement. Yet, his courage to ask the question caused him to make radical changes in his church that have led to renewed growth and kingdom progress as this church is now reaching people far from God.

"Why do people come to this church?" This is such an important question and one that isn't asked often enough. When a leader realizes why people attend his church, the church either finds their unique position in the community or discovers a problem that needs to be fixed. If the reason people are attending is that your church is geared exclusively for Christians, you need to make some adjustments. If people attend your church because they're far from God, and your church is where they feel comfortable enough to explore the claims of Jesus, then you know you're on track.

"Am I pushing the ball up the field?" This question speaks to the effectiveness of the leader. I ask myself this question almost every day. I want to make sure that every day I'm working, I am actively working towards our goals and objectives. Average leaders are content just to be active all day long. Above average leaders are concerned with effectiveness.

"What's distracting me?" This question can uncover problems that we're dealing with, but aren't recognizing as challenges. When I'm having problems with a staff member, it causes me to be distracted. If you asked me how things are, I'd say "fine." Yet, when I slow down enough to ask what's distracting me, I discover

the things that are keeping me up at night. Usually, we know what we have to do, we just don't want to do it, and that's why we're distracted.

"What am I pretending not to know?" Several years ago, I had a staff member who was severely unhappy with his position on our staff. My staff was working around him to get things done, his performance was subpar, and I didn't even want to talk to him because it was always a problem. Yet, I was pretending not to know he was unhappy. It was easier for me to bury my head in the sand and pretend everything was OK because to acknowledge that something was wrong was to invite awkward conversations and difficult decisions into my life. Yet when I confronted the issue and dealt with it, the process was hard, but the result was a better working environment for our staff.

"Where's my time/energy going?" I am a freak about managing my time. I hate when my time is wasted, and I work hard not to waste the time of others. Yet, leaders need to make sure the activities in which they engage aren't wasting their time. I realized this a couple of years ago when I reviewed my week and realized how much time I had given to work that should have been delegated. I decided to take some tasks off my plate and give them to others. The result was more focus and less clutter in my life. Yet, this type of focus doesn't happen without moments of reflection and asking ourselves this question.

"Am I focused on my strengths?" All leaders have tasks to perform that are outside of their strengths. For example, leading meetings are not a forte of mine, yet as the senior pastor, there are meetings I must lead. My concern here is for you to make

sure the majority of your time is spent doing what you do best. Are you spending 80 percent of your time doing what only you can do? If you are, you're setting yourself up for success. If you aren't, you're probably frustrating your staff, co-workers, and your church because people with those strengths would love to help you if you would only ask.

"Am I intentionally developing other leaders?" Leadership development is an area of ministry that usually doesn't have people screaming and calling us to focus on it. Instead, it is a vital area of church that can easily be neglected. I like to get even more specific when asking this question. I like to ask, "Who are the people whose leadership abilities I've developed in the last six months?" You can't lie about it when you have to make a list of names. This question helps me stay intentional about reproducing leaders and investing in people who want to grow.

"Am I growing?" Only you can answer this question. Most of us can fake it pretty well, but we know if we are growing or not. It's very easy to coast along and ride the growth of the past. Here's where I can see if I'm growing or not in my preaching. If my preaching is getting stale, if I'm using the same illustrations, if I'm coming back to the same topics and hobbyhorses, then I know something is wrong. Personal and spiritual growth brings life and vitality to preaching and communicating. We all go through dry seasons, but a commitment to growth brings us out of these times and gives us a message to share from that dry experience.

"Am I still passionate about what I'm doing?" Every year, I ask myself if I still want to be the senior pastor of Calvary Fellowship.

Some think I'm crazy to ask this question, but I believe it's vital. The last thing my church needs is a pastor who doesn't want to be there. Many times, when a person begins to lose passion, it's not a sin issue per se; it's a sign that God is working and is ready to reveal a new assignment to him. I like to check myself and make sure I'm still passionate about reaching lost people in Miami with the Gospel. Does that mean I don't get discouraged? Of course, I do. I have thought of quitting more times than I'd like to admit. But I would never allow myself to make a decision like that simply based on emotion alone. Instead, I ask, "Why am I discouraged?" Usually, it's because I am so passionate about reaching people far from God, and things aren't going the way I had hoped. So, I'm still passionate; I'm just frustrated with my results at that moment.

My encouragement to you is to ask yourself these questions and any others you think would keep you focused and effective for the kingdom of God. The leader who never questions himself is at best ignorant and at worst arrogant. Be a wise leader—one who is not afraid of the questions he asks, but instead fears what happens when he doesn't ask any questions at all.

CHAPTER 60
Keep Improving

"There is very little difference between one who cannot read and one who will not read."

—Jim Rohn

It is a shame to me that more people don't take personal improvement seriously. Think about these statistics from the American Booksellers Association:

80 percent of all Americans did not read a book this year.
70 percent of American adults have not been in a bookstore in the last five years.
58 percent of Americans never read a book after high school.
42 percent of university graduates never read another book.

Another study reports that only 14 percent of people actually go into a bookstore and leave with a book in their hands.

Shockingly, only 10 percent of those people actually read past the first chapter.

What do these statistics tell you? They tell me that most people aren't concerned with improving themselves. Instead, they're concerned with comfort and ease. People who read at all spend about two hours reading a week. Yet, the average American spends 2,000 hours a year watching television. Why do I give you all of these data? I write them to tell you that standing out isn't hard if you're willing to do some work. People today ask their bosses for raises simply because another year has gone by, not because they have increased their value in their company through learning new skills. So, what I want to give you are my *five ways to keep improving and investing in yourself.*

Challenge yourself. A few years ago, I accepted an invitation to speak at a couples retreat. I was looking forward to it, until I read the fine print in the e-mail requesting me to speak—the message I was supposed to deliver had to be in Spanish! Now, I'm of Cuban descent and am fluent in Spanish but ordering black beans and rice at a restaurant and teaching the Bible in Spanish are not the same things. I was ready to cancel when I thought, "When was the last time I challenged myself like this?" So, with the help of a friend, I took the message I was going to give in English and translated it into Spanish (it's amazing how some jokes don't work in other languages).

You and I grow when we challenge ourselves. So, put yourself in situations where you will grow. When I was first starting in ministry, I made a rule that I would never say no to a funeral. It was an area in which I needed to grow. That first year, I officiated over thirty funerals. Today, officiating funerals is not a difficult task for me. Yet, had I not challenged myself, I would still be stumbling over my words and not confident in a time of people's deepest hurt.

1 percent improvement. What would it take you to improve what you do by 1 percent? Could you preach better by 1 percent? Could you lead better by 1 percent? Could you be 1 percent more efficient with your time? I think all of us could find a way to be 1 percent better. If we decided to do that this week, then next week, and then the week after, do you know what would happen after a year? We would be 52 percent better than we were a year ago. The Japanese call this principle *Kaizen*. It means to make small improvements or, literally, "good change." Too often, we think we have to overhaul our lives completely, and that's what keeps us from making any changes. Instead, think small. What is one change you could make today? Make that change, and make another tomorrow. Improve by 1 percent, and after time, you will see drastic improvement in your life.

Always be learning. I've touched on this in previous chapters, but I want to give this practical note: always be learning. That means if you have an appointment with your doctor, take a book with you. Don't be like everyone else who's reading a 1997 copy of People magazine with Milli Vanilli on the cover. Instead, use that time to learn. In your car, stop listening to talk radio. Trust me, the morning shows have nothing to offer but mindless chatter. Instead, use the time in your car as an opportunity to grow and learn. Bring your headphones with you to the gym, and listen to something that's going to stretch your mind while you're building your muscles. I have a rule that, unless I'm out with my family, I want to have a book in my hand. I actually take books with me on driving trips just in case my car breaks down, and I have to wait for AAA.

Get around people who challenge you. International speaker Charlie "Tremendous" Jones says, "Five years from now, you'll be the same person you are today except for the people you meet and the books you read." That's a powerful statement. If you want to grow continually as a leader, you need to get around leaders who are ahead of you. You need to ask them great questions. Here's what I've learned: most leaders are happy to meet with other leaders. Very few leaders are actually calling and asking for thirty minutes of their time to learn from them. Most are too proud to humble themselves and ask questions, and the majority of those that remain are too shy to ask. This puts you in an elite group of learners who want to learn. Make a point to meet with a leader you can learn from at least once a month. Think about the net gain of wisdom, knowledge, and insight you could gain in a year through twelve meetings with high capacity leaders. It could transform your leadership.

Commit never to stop growing. Everything in life begins with a commitment. Once you commit to growing as a leader, commit never to stop growing as a leader. No one can force you to grow. Only you can take the steps necessary to become a great leader by making great leadership your highest aim. So, attend the conferences where great leadership is taught, read and re-read the books that share the principles of outstanding leadership, and move around leaders who can model what great leadership looks like.

Leadership isn't just about leading others. Leadership starts with leading yourself. Once you can master leading yourself, leading others is much easier.

CHAPTER 61
Starbucks-Style Marketing to Your Community

Tall. Grande. Venti. This is common speak for every coffee drinker who darkens the door of his or her local Starbucks. What I find amusing is that each of these words means the same—big. However, to the world who has not walked into Howard Shultz's house of coffee beans, these words don't make sense. Yet, it takes only one visit before you order your first "decaf, iced, triple grande, vanilla, 2% extra whip, three Splenda, upside-down, white mocha."

Then, you're initiated. Many people have this experience at churches when they visit for the first time. Someone hears unfamiliar theological terms, but after a season, he strikes a conversation about penal substitutionary atonement or the Holy Spirit's sanctifying work.

Yet, here's what I have noticed about Starbucks that you should implement in your church. Starbucks never uses their insider terms in their marketing pieces. Instead, they use common terms that connect with even the occasional coffee drinker. In their marketing pieces, Starbucks uses words such as *coffee, beverage,* and *morning cup* to describe their offerings. Once people are inside the coffee house, Starbucks brings out the phrases that solidify their brand and make the outsiders feel as if they've been initiated into the group.

Starbucks marketing is effective because they speak the language of the market they target. Churches must learn to do the same. We need to explain what we do as a church in words the unchurched people in our community understand and that move them.

I once received a flyer on my door that used nothing but church language. It said, "Are you tired of churches that don't talk enough about being 'washed in the blood,' 'justified in the spirit,' and 'sanctified by the Holy Ghost'?" This flyer was so filled with church language that a person needed a theology degree to fully understand it.

This approach is wrong if your goal is to reach those in your community who don't know God. You won't reach people if you don't speak their language. The more you speak in terms they understand, the more they connect with you. So instead of saying, "We're a church that preaches the true Gospel without compromise," you might want to write, "We're a church where you can connect with God and learn more about Him." It's not that the first phrase is wrong, and the second is right; unchurched people have no idea what the former statement means.

Chip and Dan Heath, in their book, *Made to Stick,* have a section called, "The Curse of Knowledge." They describe this through a simple activity where you tap the rhythm to a song on your desk and have someone guess what the song is. The other person never gets it right. Why? It is because the person listening can't hear the melody in your head. He or she hears only the tapping.

The goal is to write copy in your marketing pieces for those who don't yet hear the song. These people don't have the Christian background, Bible education, or experience in church you have, which means you need to take the time to write words they understand.

Contemporary churches believe they have learned the lesson while traditional churches are guilty of their marketing sin. However, I have learned that contemporary churches can violate this principle just as much as traditional churches. Younger churches say things such as, "Come hear our great worship." As Christians, we know that worship means *music.* However, the typical unchurched person does not. So, in your marketing, if you want to talk about the music at your church, you need to use the word music to not confuse them with insider language.

We didn't become experts at this overnight, but the more we have improved and tried to get into the minds of those far from God in our community, the greater our impact has been through our marketing efforts. Your church has a message your community must hear. So, speak the language your community understands, so they can attend, and they can be transformed by the Gospel's power. Then, you'll watch and see their cup runneth over.

CHAPTER 62
The Tale of Two Karate Studios

I was introduced to martial arts at an early age. I watched every Bruce Lee movie with cult-like devotion. I finally talked my mom into signing me up for karate classes at 10, and I loved it. My instructor's name was Tony, and he was the toughest man I had ever met. He was a third-degree black belt who regularly told us stories of fights he got into while pumping gas or shopping in the grocery store.

Tony was tough on his students, and his classes were not fun by entertainment standards, but I learned to defend myself. I never feared walking home alone on the mean streets of Boston because Tony taught me how to take care of business, if necessary.

This isn't to say that, as 10-, 11-, and 12-year-olds, we didn't complain about Tony's teaching style. We complained all the time. Other karate studios had much more fun during classes. Tony was all business, teaching us what we needed to know to reach the next level and ultimately earn a black belt.

Within two years, I had climbed to a brown belt, and I was two levels away from my black belt when the unthinkable happened—Tony was fired. The karate studio's owner wanted to change the studio's climate and make it more fun, so he hired two guys who had studied under Tony to run the classes.

At first, it was amazing! We sparred in every class. We did all the fun activities Tony never allowed us to do. Then, I noticed something; I hadn't progressed any closer to my goal of becoming a black belt. Instead, I was stuck. Months went by, and I started to forget some forms (patterns of movements) I had learned under Tony's teaching. I brought this to the attention of the new instructors, and they ignored it because the classes were growing, and everyone was having fun. Not long after that, I quit karate, never to return.

At a young age, I learned the tension most church leaders feel. There's the desire to teach people what they need to know, while trying to present messages in a way people want to hear. No pastor wants to sound like a boring college professor, but no one learns how to live by listening to a stand-up comedian. I've learned that we must live in the struggle. To relieve the pressure is to give way to either side, and that's not healthy.

Solomon wrote, *"The Preacher sought to find acceptable words; and what was written was upright—words of truth"* (Ecc. 12:10 NKJV). There's tension in this verse. The preacher is looking for acceptable words. In the Hebrew language, *acceptable* can also be translated "delightful, pleasurable, and desirous." He wants to present truth interestingly and palatably. Every pastor goes through this struggle as he prepares to teach God's Word.

To veer too far into scholarly realms is to preach as Tony taught his classes—like a drill sergeant giving orders. He gave little thought to your feelings or problems. On the other side was the karate studio run by the guys who wanted everyone to just have a good time. It was great for a while, but no one was progressing to maturity. Everyone showed up to feel good, but there was no real growth.

The best churches don't swing to either side, but try to live in the middle of both places. They want to present truth without compromise, but they want that truth communicated interestingly, which is a more difficult way to teach. It's easy to write a Bible college-level lecture. It's easy to stand and tell a few jokes. It takes real skill and gifting to present solid, biblical teaching and present it in a way that holds people's attention for a long period. But when you can find that balance, there's no stopping your teaching and ministry.

CHAPTER 63
Greenroom Pastors

I love the greenroom. Every pastor does. Your favorite breakfast foods are there. Your favorite energy drinks and bottled waters are fully stocked. There's a comfortable spot for you to sit and study. You're away from the crowd... but that's the problem.

The greenroom used to be where the pastor could collect his thoughts and look over his notes before preaching. Now, the pastor hides there from the congregation.

A few years ago, I found myself having little contact with my congregation because I "studied" in the greenroom. I had to get out of the greenroom because I was out of touch with people. So, I decided to sit in the front row in every service and worship before I taught.

Let me share what I've learned...

1. I Became a Worship Leader

When I got out of the greenroom and sat in the crowd with the rest of the church, the congregation started to watch how I worship. I heard frustration from leaders and staff about how the men didn't engage in worship. I realized it's because none of the male leadership in the church was in the auditorium during worship.

Let's fast-forward three months. Twelve Sundays after I started to sit in the front row and worship with the church, the men were lifting their hands and singing loudly. They saw their pastor worship, and they saw that as the model for how they should worship. The day we get out of the greenroom and get in the auditorium, we become worship leaders.

2. I Started to Prepare My Heart

In the greenroom, I looked over my notes and prepared my message. When I started to worship the Lord before I preached, I started to prepare my heart, which was a game changer for me. I began to see my message as connected to the rest of the service. (I know we all say it's connected, but few believe it). Most of us see the message as the main course and the music as the appetizer. I know we deny that publicly, but many of us think it. I did… and I was wrong.

My preaching got better when I stopped looking at the notes and started to look at the Lord before I preached.

3. I Experienced the Entire Service

If you're a greenroom pastor, you experience only the part of the service you participate in—the message. When you get out of the greenroom, you see everything people experience. Today, when I preach, I usually open by commenting on what previously happened in the service. This way, we make the service not one collective experience, but three or four loosely connected, independent units.

4. I Realized I Was Ready to Preach

I used to hide in the greenroom under the guise of "I need a few minutes to make some final changes to the message." Here's what I know now: If I'm not ready to preach my message when I arrive at church, 10 minutes in the greenroom won't change it.

Here's my encouragement to you—leave the greenroom. Get out among the people you teach, and lead. Teach them to worship the Lord. Show them that worship isn't the 15 minutes they have to get to church before the message starts. It's when God prepares the soil of our hearts to receive the Word's seed.

Here's how strongly I feel about this: Our building under construction won't have a greenroom. I don't need one. As long as there's an empty seat in the auditorium, there's a spot for me.

CHAPTER 64
How to Juggle while Preaching

I want to dispel a misconception in the church—that a pastor cannot disciple the congregation and evangelize the lost in the same service. This philosophy led to the Seeker Movement in the seventies and eighties. The strategy back then was to have a service for believers (usually a midweek Bible study) and then reserve the weekend for the unchurched to hear the Gospel. Many churches saw amazing growth using this dual approach, and many people were converted as a result. The chief reason for implementing this game plan was that it was too difficult to do discipleship and evangelism in the same service.

This has changed in today's cultural landscape. So much so, it's vital that we disciple believers and evangelize lost people simultaneously. The question is, "How can we aim at two targets and hit both without muddying the waters for each?" I have found that expository preaching can strengthen the believer and challenge the non-Christian toward a decision for Christ. How is this possible? I have noted three ways expository preaching accomplishes this goal.

Expository Preaching Emphasizes the Bible

Both believers and nonbelievers are interested to know what the Bible has to say. Sometimes, we forget that people decide to go to church because something in their life causes them to seek answers to the most important questions in life. So, when a pastor stands and teaches verse by verse through the Bible, the emphasis changes from what the pastor thinks to what the Bible says.

Expository Preaching Creates Trust with the Unchurched

When a pastor primarily teaches topically, the unchurched person looks on and says, "Is that what the Bible really says, or is this preacher making it say what he wants?" When a pastor preaches verse by verse through a section of scripture, unchurched people accept what is said because they read each verse with the pastor.

We minister to thousands of unchurched people yearly at Calvary, the church I pastor. One of the most frequent comments we receive is about our style of expository preaching. People say, "I felt like the message was so simple and straight from the Bible." People feel that there's no funny business when the pastor works his way through the text without jumping around from one end of the Bible to the other.

Expository Preaching Forces You to Remember the Audience

When a pastor preaches through challenging verses in the Bible, he is forced to think about an unchurched person's response. When preaching through Ephesians 5 and talking about wives submitting to their husbands, pastors must think about how a nonbeliever will respond to this passage. Some will think, "Passages such as this cause me not to be a Christian. I cannot get past antiquated ideas such as this."

Here's the reality—you need to answer this question when teaching this passage, not only because non-Christians are in the audience, but also because Christians in the crowd think the same or have friends who question this teaching. She wants to hear your explanation so she can have an answer for her friend. Expository preaching forces preachers to talk about uncomfortable subjects and deal with them head on. When we do, we answer the questions of unbelievers and disciple the believers who listen.

Expository preaching is more difficult than topical preaching is. Yet, if you want to disciple the church and reach the unchurched, I don't know of a better method to hit both targets.

CHAPTER 65
Conference Syndrome

I want you to imagine the scene: The pastor has just finished attending the latest leadership conference rife with new ideas and the latest breakthrough growth techniques. You can't read minds, but you know what he's thinking: "I will change everything the moment I get home!"

How do I know what this pastor is plotting? It's because I used to be him. My staff used to fear my attending a conference because everything I saw seemed better than what I was doing. I tried to implement everything I saw, and the result was a disaster.

I have attended many conferences, and they have inspired me at different levels in my ministry. Yet, before I make a paradigm shift with a ministry, program, or idea, and "plug and play," I need to consider three important factors that will determine its success or failure:

1. Will It Work in My Local Culture?

I attended a conference a few years ago that challenged every church leader to put huge amounts of time, energy, and resources into a Christmas Eve service. They said they had all the data about how Christmas Eve was a better opportunity to reach the unchurched, and I believed them. I didn't think they would lie to me, and after all, they had data. So, I went home and did what they told me. I put time, effort, energy, and many resources into our Christmas Eve services, only to be sorely disappointed.

So what did I do? Give up? Not a chance! The next year, we put more effort, more energy, more resources… and we got similar results. I felt like such a failure. Christmas Eve works for everyone, except a loser like me. How could Christmas Eve not work for us?

As I started to think about our local culture, things became clearer. Christmas Eve in Miami, with the huge Latin population, is a sacred family day. Noche Buena, as we call it, is to Hispanics what Thanksgiving Day is to Americans. It is a family day on which everyone cooks, eats, and celebrates. Christmas Eve in a Hispanic home is much more significant than Christmas Day is.

We started to conduct services on the days leading up to Christmas Eve, and the response was amazing. You must consider your local culture before implementing big changes in your church.

LEADERSHIP BLURBS

2. **Do You Have the Talent to Make It Happen?**

   Years ago, live drama was all the rage in church circles. I went to a conference that highlighted their drama teams, and I was thoroughly impressed. The skits I saw were as good as anything I saw on NBC or CBS.

   I got back to my church, and my one goal was to implement the drama ministry I had seen. Here was the problem: I didn't have any good actors in the church with a heart for this type of ministry. So although I tried to coax people to "give it a try," it was a disaster.

   After a season of trying desperately to make this happen, we let it go. We didn't have the talent then to make it work. So, we decided to implement what we had, which were talented video production people. Our videos are topnotch and cutting edge, but the best part is that the videos are not forced; they are the overflow of the talent God has brought us, and we can use the arts to connect creatively with those who visit our Calvary Fellowship.

3. **Extract the Universal Principle**

   When you hear a conference speaker say that some style of music was a key to reaching many people, be careful. However, don't throw the baby out with the bathwater. Extract the universal principle, which might be, "We expect excellence in our music department." But don't play country music just because someone said that worked in his or her church. A wise leader takes the principle and allows that to help him go to the next level.

CONCLUSION
Leadership that Climbs Mountains

On a recent family vacation to Disney World, our family decided to rent Surrey bikes and ride around the Disney resorts. If you aren't familiar with Surrey bikes, several people can pedal these bikes together.

My oldest daughter had asked all week if we could rent a bike, so on the last day, I reluctantly agreed. I put my oldest daughter Mia (4) and my son Xander (2) in the front area where younger kids sit, and my (seven-months pregnant) wife and me in the back to pedal in unison.

I love Disney, but I don't think anyone in upper management has pedaled the trail mapped for us. There were two significant hills to climb, and after the first, my wife and I looked at each other as if death were just around the bend.

We reached the second hill, my legs burned, and I turned to my wife Carey and said, "My legs feel like they're on fire." We finally made it one full lap around the lake, and Mia said, "Let's go one more time." Before I could exert my parental authority and say, "No way!" my wife said, "Of course, sweetheart."

We started lap two, and when we reached the first hill, Carey said, "Robert, I'm pregnant; I can't pedal anymore." So, she stopped pedaling. For those keeping score at home, I was the only one pedaling, and I had three people freeloading on my bike. Through sheer force of will, I pedaled up the first hill. However, when we reached the second hill, I didn't have the strength to make it to the top. My wife lovingly said, "Bob, it's OK; I'll walk." I responded, "But honey, you're pregnant... OK, get off!"

She got off the bike, but I still couldn't make it up the hill. Then, from nowhere, I got the biggest burst of Herculean strength I have ever known, and I start to dominate the hill I'm climbing. I turned around to tell Carey about my explosion of strength when I realized that she was pushing the bike! I didn't like the picture of my seven-months pregnant wife pushing us uphill, and I wanted her to stop. However, what came of my mouth was, "Keep pushing!" The worst part of this entire fiasco was that as all this happened, a family of four (all pedaling in harmony) was pedaling up the hills, laughing the whole time... at me.

Sometimes, leadership seems as though you're pedaling uphill. It seems nearly impossible, and no one is helping you up the hill. Then, you look at others, and it seems easy for them. So, you conclude there must be something wrong with you.

There's nothing wrong with you. Leadership is difficult. It's not impossible, but it is the most challenging endeavor you will ever undertake. So, here's my encouragement to you—keep pedaling.

When you want to give up, keep pedaling. When things don't

work out how you hoped, keep pedaling. God brings the right people at the right time to help you get where you need to go, as long as you keep pedaling.

Endnotes

[i] Jim Loehr and Tony Schwartz, *The Power of Full Engagement: Managing Energy, Not Time, Is the Key to High Performance and Personal Renewal* (New York: Free Press, 2003), 4.

[ii] Jim Rohn The Art of Exceptional Living Audio Series 2003

[iii] Brian Tracy Success Mastery Academy Audio Series 2005

[iv] Edison on Innovation by Alan Axelrod Jossey-Bass (San Francisco, CA) 2008

[v] Brian Tracy, *Hire and Keep the Best People: 21 Practical & Proven Techniques You Can Use Immediately!* (San Francisco: Berrett-Koehler Publishers, 2001), 49.

[vi] Bill Hybels Courageous Leadership Zondervan Publishers (Grand Rapids, MI) 2002 Pg. 80-84

[vii] Tom Kelley The Ten Faces of Innovation Doubleday Business (New York, NY) 2005 Pg. 75

[viii] For a detailed discussion of "The Win," *see Seven Practices for Effective Ministry* by Andy Stanley and Reggie Joiner.

[ix] Andy Stanley Fields of Gold Tyndale House Publishing (Wheaton, IL) 2004

[x] Patrick Lencioni Jossey-Bass (San Francisco, CA) 2004

[xi] Jim Collins Good to Great Harper Collins (New York, NY) 2001 Pg. 13

[xii] Tracy, Brian Goals! *How to Get Everything You Want--Faster Than You Ever Thought Possible* (Berrett-Koehler Publishers 2004)

[xiii] Jim Rohn 2004 Leadership Weekend event Audio Series

[xiv] Genett, Donna *If you want it done right, you don't have to do it yourself* (Quill Driver Books 2003)

[xv] Winget, Larry *Shut Up, Stop Whining and Get a Life: A Kick Butt Approach to a Better Life* (Wiley Publishing 2005) Page 107

EVANGELISM NINJA
HELPING PASTORS SUCCEED

If you're tired of throwing away thousands of dollars on outreach and want to see your church grow from 21%-35% this year, **then test drive Evangelism Ninja for just $1.**

Evangelism Ninja focuses on the 7 Secrets to Effective Outreach:

1. Evangelistic Culture
2. Targeted Market
3. Trackable Results
4. Eye-Catching Design
5. Effective follow-up
6. Healthy Team
7. Strategic Budgeting

> Visit evangelismninja.com and take the
> **TESTDRIVE for $1**

Follow Bob Franquiz:
Twitter: @bobfranquiz
Facebook: fb.com/bfranquiz
Instagram: bobfranquiz

www.evangelismninja.com

Leadership Ninja is a step by step program that gives you all the tools you need to develop leaders at every level and see them grow to maturity.

What's Covered in Leadership Ninja?

1. Leadership Development from the Ground Up
2. The Art of Strategic Investment
3. Turning Your Audience Into an Army
4. Leading Yourself
5. Building Your Dream Team
6. Coaching a Championship Caliber Team
7. The Science of Casting Vision
8. Evaluating Your Team
9. Laying A Solid Foundation
10. Dollars and Sense

Visit leadershipninja.com and take the
TESTDRIVE for $1

Follow Bob Franquiz:
Twitter: @bobfranquiz
Facebook: fb.com/bfranquiz
Instagram: bobfranquiz

www.leadershipninja.com